A GUIDE
TO
WRITING
SOCIAL
STORIES™

A GUIDE TO WRITING SOCIAL STORIES™

Step-by-Step Guidelines for Parents and Professionals

Chris Williams
and Barry Wright

Jessica Kingsley *Publishers*
London and Philadelphia

First published in 2017
by Jessica Kingsley Publishers
73 Collier Street
London N1 9BE, UK
and
400 Market Street, Suite 400
Philadelphia, PA 19106, USA

www.jkp.com

Library of Congress Cataloging in Publication Data
Names: Williams, Chris, 1955- author. | Wright, Barry, author.
Title: A guide to writing social stories : step-by-step guidelines for
    parents and professionals / Chris Williams and Barry Wright.
Description: London ; Philadelphia : Jessica Kingsley Publishers, 2017. |
    Includes bibliographical references and index.
Identifiers: LCCN 2016027410 | ISBN 9781785921216 (alk. paper)
Subjects: LCSH: Composition (Language arts)--Therapeutic use. | Creative
    writing--Therapeutic use. | Autism in children--Psychological aspects.
Classification: LCC RJ505.C64 W55 2017 | DDC 618.92/891663--dc23 LC record available at
https://urldefense.proofpoint.com/v2/url?u=https-3A__lccn.loc.gov_2016027410&d=BQIFAg&
c=euGZstcaTDllvimEN8b7jXrwqOf-v5A_CdpgnVfiiMM&r=VCKr2NBFNTs4O_kp07esGY2J-
doQEb4zTq5sCaeXa-I&m=tlJHyDKe8gwn4O_wydJAjFG7hrpxDzpQnyZniIlg6to&s=Fto4bJK
ZcAx-apurpXHH_a1kHaYNv4jB1CzR9WlVERo&e=

British Library Cataloguing in Publication Data
A CIP catalogue record for this book is available from the British Library

ISBN 978 1 78592 121 6
eISBN 978 1 78450 388 8

Printed and bound in Great Britain

CONTENTS

Part 4   More Examples of Social Stories

Part 5   Appendices

FOREWORD: A PARENT'S VIEW

As a parent of a child with autism, I am proud to have been involved in workshops to inform the writing of this guide. My first thought is that all children are unique, and this book respects that vision, providing a clear and easy-to-use guide to Carol Gray's Social Stories.

Every young person is special, with a unique combination of abilities and needs which affect learning. All young people deserve the opportunity to learn in ways that make the most of their strengths. Children with autism and Asperger syndrome are individuals with their own hopes, likes and dislikes, skills, interests and passions.

Young people who have autism (and are aware of this) may be teased and they may draw attention away from it or be under pressure to 'fit in'. We need to make sure that they have the support, understanding and tolerance they deserve.

As adults it is important to think about the young person's ordinary needs for love, closeness, touch, security, fun and laughter, friends, achievement, respect, hope and a sense of being wanted for who they are.

Some thoughts for parents and teachers to consider: are there particular interests or skills that could be turned into a gift? For example, Jack can sometimes be distracted by someone wearing glasses or earrings – does he have an eye for detail and notice small differences? Mona spends a lot of time straightening her desk and putting things away – is she organised and tidy?

Respect for individual rights and needs is enshrined in law. For example, the Disability Discrimination Act 1995 and the Equality Act 2010 both lay out clear principles in law that all parents, teachers and society at large must follow. It is very important to know this because it will affect the day-to-day work of teachers, and will ensure the needs of children with autism or Asperger syndrome are being met.

This makes sure that young people with autism are not discriminated against. In education, for example, this includes thinking about:

- changes to practices or procedures

- changes to physical features

- changes to how learners are assessed

- providing extra support and aids (such as specialist teachers or equipment).

Social Stories can help with this in unseen ways. They are a process that enables us to understand our children better. They prompt us to work together to explore what *we* can do rather than trying to get the young person with autism to change something that is a result of their impairment.

Used properly, Social Stories are a great force for positive development. This is not just through the Social Story itself but in the empowering process that leads to the Story, the detective work, talking to the child or young person themselves and all those who know them and working together in a supportive alliance. Indeed, as a parent and educationalist, I have found most value in the setting up of Social Stories (including those deemed 'unsuccessful') in giving me a different perspective of a situation I thought I had understood well.

This guide will help parents, teachers and other adults supporting a child to write and use Social Stories. I commend it to you.

Jo Whitehead (parent)

ACKNOWLEDGEMENTS

We would like to thank many people for their support and wonderful contributions throughout the various stages of the writing of this guide. Huge thanks to the Lime Trees research team and the York University researchers who conducted the systematic review of Social Stories and the qualitative work (interviews and focus groups) with parents, young people, teachers and clinicians. Their work formed the foundation of this guide. Thanks also to the parents and professionals who attended meetings to advise and guide us throughout the 3-year research period and the schools and individuals who were participants in the research trial to test Social Stories in 37 different schools. With special thanks to David Marshall who was Trial Co-ordinator for the research, displaying great patience and perseverance. Also a big thank you to all of the teachers and parents and young people who generously shared their fantastic Social Stories with us and gave permission for them to appear in this guide. Elaine Robinson and her daughter Isabel very kindly agreed to star in the online video clip that accompanies this guide and gave us six of their Stories, which appear in Part 4. Thanks also to Gill Callaghan, who edited our final version.

Finally, a very large thank you to Carol Gray. Her Social Stories have in our opinion been one of the most successful interventions for children and young people with autism in the last 25 years. She very kindly agreed to support this research and to advise us during the writing of this guide. She helped us to write the checklist that operationalises her ten defining criteria for Social Stories (10.2 criteria, Gray 2015). This will become a very useful tool for those wishing to write and check their Social Stories but also a tool for use in future research. Thank you!

INTRODUCTION

This guide was written for professionals and parents as a guide to writing Social Stories. It was developed as part of a large research study to evaluate the effectiveness of Social Stories in helping young people with autism and Asperger syndrome in mainstream schools in the United Kingdom (Autism Spectrum Social Stories in Schools Trial (ASSSIST), Wright *et al.* 2014; Marshall *et al.* 2016; Wright *et al.* 2016).

Carol Gray introduced Social Stories over 25 years ago. They have been used widely and are perceived by many to have been one of the most effective ways of helping young people with autism to understand their social environment more successfully. Social Stories provide information about specific social situations in order to increase understanding for children and young people. This often leads to the secondary effect of a Social Story, which is a positive change in the child's life and reduced anxiety and distress.

This guide is based on the 10.2 revised criteria (Gray 2015) and is divided into five parts.

Part 1 provides information about autism and Asperger syndrome with the aim of helping the reader to understand how young people with autism spectrum disorder (ASD) may see and experience the world they live in. It also includes some of the background to Social Stories and an explanation of why they are particularly relevant in this situation.

Part 2 takes a step-by-step approach to writing Social Stories with the British audience particularly in mind. This section was written in consultation with parents and teachers who have had experience with using Social Stories in practice and with a great deal of support and advice from Carol Gray. There is a worked example in this section called 'Taking turns to help in assembly'.

Part 3 contains further examples of the process of writing Social Stories, including how to gather information for the Story.

Part 4 is a collection of completed Stories written by parents and teachers involved in the study.

Part 5 contains extra resources including a template for gathering information, a flowchart, some very useful checklists and a list of definitions of terms.

There is a video to accompany this guide, which is a summary of Social Stories as described by Isabel and her mum and one of the authors. It was filmed in 2014. Many thanks to them for sharing their experiences! Go to: https://youtu.be/V1x7i7HfVow

Part 1

SOCIAL STORIES
and Autism

1

UNDERSTANDING AUTISM

Autism spectrum disorder (ASD) is a developmental disorder that normally becomes evident in the first 3 years of a child's life. It includes autism, Asperger syndrome and atypical autism. ASD affects communication, social interaction, imagination and behaviour. It is not something a child can catch.

Parents do not cause it.

All children with ASD will continue to make developmental progress and there is a great deal that can be done to help. The following sections describe some important theories that help explain it in more detail.

Mindblindness

Children with ASD are delayed in developing Theory of Mind and struggle to learn it intuitively in everyday interactions in the same way other children do. Some books call this mindblindness. Mindblindness refers to being partially blind to understanding the minds of other people. Consequently, people with ASD have great difficulty in understanding the point of view, thoughts or feelings of someone else. Mindblindness leads to great difficulties in making accurate guesses about what people might be thinking or feeling or in predicting what they are going to do. This is a crucial skill for successful social interactions.

Imagine being unable to understand how someone else is thinking or feeling; imagine not being able to consider their point of view. How confusing and frightening the world must seem and how difficult social interactions must be. It is not surprising, therefore, that young people on the autism spectrum are sometimes anxious, see things more from their own point of view and behave differently from other children. This is not the same as selfishness. It is a problem in their understanding of other people.

Mindblindness is not an 'all or nothing' concept. The ability to intuit another person's emotional state varies in people with or without autism. However, in children with autism, this ability is likely to be within a lower range or band and develop at a slower pace.

How does mindblindness affect children's behaviour?

- *Making poor eye contact with people.* Typically, people rely heavily on eye contact and facial expression for non-verbal social communication. A teacher may look at a child with a stern facial expression to mean 'stop doing something' but the child with ASD may be less able to understand that the eye contact or facial expression conveys meaning, or unable to interpret it because of mindblindness. The child is not (necessarily!) deliberately ignoring his or her teacher.

- *Not readily understanding or using gestures.* Gestures (such as pointing, beckoning, waving or making a 'shhh' gesture with their finger to mean 'be quiet') are a common form of non-verbal communication which are both inexact in meaning and requiring of a degree of intuition to interpret. It is less likely that a child with ASD will understand the meaning of an adult's gestures or use them themselves.

- *Friendships.* Children on the autism spectrum make friendships in different ways from many children. They are less likely to have large friendship groups and make friends more around specific interests. Mindblindness makes complex social relationships in groups more difficult.

- *Not showing the teacher or parents their drawings or work unless asked to.* Children without ASD generally show things for praise, encouragement or approval. This behaviour relies on understanding that the other person might be interested or give praise. This understanding is not necessarily present in children with ASD.

- *A lack of awareness of social conventions or what they are for.* For example, leaving the classroom to go to see the clock in the hall without realising the teacher might be worried about a missing child or that the other children are all in 'reading time'.

- *Finding it much harder to share than other children.* Sharing skills develop as a child tunes into the needs of other people. Mindblindness may mean that children with ASD struggle to understand the needs of others intuitively or that they need to share information about their own needs.

- *Lack of awareness of others' feelings (e.g. pain or distress).* Having less understanding of how their behaviour might upset others.

- *Struggling to have a two-way conversation.* They may want to talk more about their interests and be less interested in other people's hobbies or ideas.

Social Stories can be used to give children information about social situations or how others may behave.

Getting the gist

Our brains are constantly being bombarded with information. We see, hear, smell, taste and touch things. We can take in all this sensory information and make sense of it. We manage to ignore irrelevant information (like a tractor in a field, a ticking clock or the humming of the power station next door) and build all the sensory information into a clear understanding of what is going on. We have an ability to draw together lots of sensory information from a situation in order to make sense of it. For example, in a picture there are lots of colours, shapes, sizes and objects. We can see the picture as a whole and observe a group of people dressed up in fine clothes and hats throwing confetti at a couple outside a church and we might guess that this is a wedding. Our brains do this very quickly and automatically. Children with ASD appear to experience great difficulty in drawing together information in this way to understand the gist of what is going on or what is expected from them. In this example, children with ASD might focus on individual details like the church bells, or the pieces of paper floating around but fail to recognise the event as a wedding. They may focus in on small details of the way something sounds, looks, feels or smells. It seems as if they 'can't see the woods for the trees'.

Similarly, young people on the autism spectrum can appear to be very literal in the understanding of verbal requests. Often this is related to their failure to 'get the gist'. For example if a teacher gave a homework exercise to the class entitled 'Was the Victorian era a golden age?' most young people would understand that they would need to write about the reasons why they agree or disagree with the question. Those with Asperger syndrome might hand in their homework with simply the answer 'Yes', and then be confused as to why their teacher was annoyed with them.

How does not being able to 'get the gist' (or understand the context) affect children's behaviour?

- *Not being able to understand that the situation or context they are in can change the meaning of some verbal requests.* For example, if a child was sitting in a classroom and a teacher said, 'Take your pencils out', most children would understand that the lesson was about to begin, whereas the child with ASD, failing to relate the words to the context, might walk out of the room with the pencils.

- *Not understanding that the teacher's instruction to the class includes them.* Children with ASD may not know about the purpose of school or the role of the teacher.

- *Interest in parts of objects rather than the whole object.* The child may see a doll's house as a series of doors, windows and walls and not play with it as a whole miniature house.

- *Focus on one aspect rather than the whole picture.* If a teacher asked the child with ASD to write about a picture of a park they had given to the child, he or she may write about the 'ladder' that forms part of the slide.

- *Not intuitively knowing how to react in social situations.* A child may push to the front of the queue when lining up to go into the classroom, not understanding that queueing is a social rule that is in place to avoid everyone rushing to the front and possibly getting hurt.

- *May learn by rote rather than intuition.* For example, one boy had to learn by extensive questioning which objects fall under the category of fruit. He went through a long period when he repeatedly asked his dad whether different items were fruit ('Is a banana fruit?' 'Is a table fruit?' 'Is a sausage fruit?'), until he had satisfied himself that he knew which items belonged to the fruit category. He struggled to 'get the gist' of 'fruit-ness' without learning the lists in his mind.

- *May not see a face as a whole but see it as elements of detail.* Research shows that children with ASD may focus on the mouth or other parts of the face and not see the whole facial expression.

- *Understanding of concepts and words.* Some children may have a particular interpretation of a word or phrase that then causes them to worry. An example of this would be a child being told he should be proud of an achievement believing this was a criticism as he knows pride to be considered a deadly sin.

Social Stories can help children get the gist (understand the context) of what is going on in some situations by describing it clearly, and filling in the gaps in children's knowledge or understanding.

Language and communication

Most infants are born with an inbuilt ability to develop communication skills. Some of the communication problems children on the autism spectrum experience may come from the difficulties described above, such as mindblindness. For example, children may not know they need to tell others when they need something. Children on the autism spectrum often have additional language difficulties. This varies very much from person to person and may be shown in a number of ways. Children with ASD may develop language later than other children and have delayed receptive (understanding what is said) and expressive (talking or signing) language skills. On the other hand, children with Asperger syndrome will have apparently normal language acquisition in infancy and problems only occur later when abstract language and social use of language are being developed. Most children with ASD have difficulties with the social use of language.

How do language and communication difficulties affect the child's behaviour?

- *Starting a conversation.* Introduction to a conversation may be unusual. For example, the child might find less than subtle ways of attracting the adult's attention such as moving the head of the person they are trying to talk to, using the adult's hand as if it were a tool, or interrupting others.

- *Difficulty talking or writing about thoughts, feelings and emotions.* Children with ASD are likely to concentrate on facts. For example, a child may be more interested in the facts about a death than the bereaved person's feelings.

- *Language may be repetitive.* Some children borrow phrases from liked films or videos. For example, a child who said, 'Come on Mumble, you can do it' (a phrase from the film *Happy Feet*) was reassuring herself that she could do a piece of work.

- *One-sided conversation.* A child with ASD may, for example, talk about their own interests and not be aware of or interested in others' responses.

- *Miscommunication and literal understanding.* The young person may misinterpret what is said. For example, they may hear, 'we're not going to the park' as 'we're going to the park' if they focus on the word 'park'. A child who is told to 'take it with a pinch of salt' may go to look for salt.

- *Sometimes 'switch off', ignore adults or seek comfort in some repetitive familiar tasks.* Understanding language requires a great deal more concentration from children with ASD than for other children. It is not surprising that they become tired and need to 'switch off' sometimes.

- *Time to process information.* Many children need to be given time to process what they are reading or hearing. Make sure you give people with ASD time to think and respond.

Imagination, time perception, planning and memory

Imagination, time perception, planning and memory are all related. Children with ASD have differences in all four areas. It is likely that differences in the way the brain approaches imagination may set up ongoing difficulties with the ability to plan things for the future and understand the passing of time.

How does difference in imagination affect the child's behaviour?

- *The way a child with ASD plays* is often different to that of typical children. Make-believe play, role play, symbolic play and imaginative use of toys are less likely except when learnt by rote or through copying others. Children with ASD often have a preference for construction toys (e.g. Lego) or the sensory aspects of toys (e.g. lining up cars). They like to organise, categorise and consolidate learnt skills. They prefer to focus time and attention on a few interests rather than lots of different new ones. They rely on memory and like to do the same things (e.g. drawing lots of similar pictures or repeating sequences of play from films or television).

- *Social problem solving and getting on with others.* Children may struggle to imagine different responses or scenarios in social situations. Social problem solving needs an ability to run scenarios in the mind to see how things might go. This leads to difficulties in social problem solving and means they may struggle to manage or repair social situations.

- *Humour.* Much humour (except slapstick) involves imagination. For example, a simple joke like 'What is yellow and dangerous?' has us imagining all sorts of possibilities before the joke teller says 'shark-infested custard'. Our imagination finds this unusual answer intriguing, unexpected, and as we try to imagine sharks in our dessert bowl or custard in the sea, it becomes humorous. The person with ASD may not find it funny because their way of thinking means they just see a shark in a dessert bowl as impossible or stupid.

- *Problems with understanding abstract concepts.* This includes difficulty understanding sarcasm, irony and abstract ideas such as heaven, trust, honour, love and freedom. People with ASD are drawn to facts and logical aspects of our world, and like consistency.

- *Social rules* are often built around abstract concepts. Most typical 10-year-olds would not say to the head teacher: 'Your car needs a wash,' because they would be able to predict that the head teacher may think it rude. However, it is not rude in itself. It depends on the circumstances and who is saying it. Social rules deem this rude for a 10-year-old, but not as a friendly aside. Most of us know this because we are intuitively aware of the unwritten social rules. These are abstract concepts. If we struggle to understand the abstract, then social rules become a problem for us.

- *Literal thinking.* With these differences in imagination a child with ASD has a predominantly logical, literal way of talking and thinking. For example, one young person with Asperger syndrome was asked to 'take a vitamin tablet in the morning'. She replied, 'Where shall I take it to?'

- *Different interests.* Having very different, unusual or specific interests may mean that they have less in common with many other children.

How does difficulty with time perception affect the child's behaviour?

- *Delay is difficult and may cause frustration.* Children with ASD often tend to live very much in the here and now. Time involves *imagining* what may be in the future. For example, if someone says, 'We are going to the hamburger restaurant at lunchtime', the child not only has to project the event into the future but also has to have a mental idea of how much time there is between now and then. They may also have to consider all the things that have to happen in the meantime.

- *Not understanding the language or concept related to a period of time*, e.g. 'lunchtime'. What is lunchtime and when is it? One father told his son at breakfast that they were going to go to the park after lunch. His son made himself a sandwich, ate it and then stood at the door waiting to go to the park because to him it was now 'after lunch'.

How does difficulty with planning affect the child's behaviour?

- *Difficulty planning.* To plan something, we have to know what the desired outcome is and to arrange in our minds a sequence of steps required to make it happen. This often involves thinking about something unknown and requires imagination, so tackling everyday problems is very difficult unless the solutions have been learnt by rote. A person with ASD will have difficulty working out the steps involved in answering many school-based problems. Even the question 'What would you like to do now?' seems overwhelming in its extent.

- *Although children with ASD are often very good at planning* when it is something they have done before, they find it hard to plan in new or different situations.

- *Planning and memory.* Because of difficulties with imagination when a parent says, 'We are going to town' a child without ASD may think of all the things he or she could do in town and consider the probabilities. The child with ASD tends to remember what they did last time 'in town'. They use their memory more than their imagination in these situations.

How does difficulty with memory affect the child's behaviour?

- *Living in the here and now.* Children with ASD often live in the here and now. If a child with ASD asks you a question and you give them an answer, they may keep on asking the same question over and over again. This may be because spoken words come and go. Unless somehow recorded, once they are spoken they are gone and hard to remember. The child may be repeatedly asking the same question as a way of understanding and remembering.

- *A preference for visual memory.* Children with ASD seem to succeed better with visual images. Recorded visual images such as charts, pictures and photographs persist and the child can refer back to them. This may be why strategies like visual social stories, visual calendars and the Picture Exchange Communication System (PECS®) work much better than equivalent spoken word-based systems.

Sensory interests, preoccupations and compulsions

For reasons not completely understood, children with ASD may develop a range of sensory interests and sensitivities. Possible explanations include the fact that children who have less ability to 'get the gist' may be less interested in overall meaning or in understanding the whole picture and so may be drawn more to the detail, or their sensory experiences. Also, differences in the way imagination is used may lead the child towards more practical, literal ways of interacting with the world. Similarly, due to mindblindness they often don't see the point of play with someone else and have a preference for solitary play. Repetitive motion or sensory play may help them relax and reduce anxiety (e.g. in social situations). Whatever the reasons, we know that children with ASD often focus on sensory experiences and that this may lead to preoccupations, compulsions or oversensitivity to sensory experiences.

- *Sensory interests.* These are interests to do with noise, touch, feel, taste, smells and/or visual experiences.

- *Preoccupations.* These are intensely held likings for activities, which go well beyond simple interests. They tend to be pursued with great enthusiasm and can be very time consuming.

- *Compulsions* are like obsessions but involve actions. A compulsion is a powerfully felt need to carry out an action or series of actions (compulsive routines), often in the same order.

- *Repetitive movements.* Some children will do things like rock, jump on the spot or spin their bodies.

How does difficulty with sensory interests or sensitivities affect the child's behaviour?

- Being distressed by certain colours, e.g. one boy was upset when his classroom door was painted red.

- Wanting to touch certain fabrics, e.g. stroking fabrics such as a cushion or other people's clothing.

- Becoming very distressed by different smells, e.g. a new perfume worn by a teacher.

- Screaming and putting hands on ears when noise is found to be unbearable, e.g. a jet flying over school.

- Running around the perimeter of the playground watching the patterns made by the fence.

How does difficulty with preoccupations affect the child's behaviour?

- A fascination for objects which occupies very large amounts of time, e.g. stamp collecting or Pokémon cards.

- Wanting to watch the same DVD repeatedly, e.g. watching the film *Toy Story* many times a day.

- A passion for collecting knowledge about things such as football stadium capacities or the history of the Titanic.

- Odd interests such as a fascination for car washes or number plates.

How does difficulty with compulsions or compulsive routines affect the child's behaviour?

- Needing to perform a routine, e.g. *having* to touch all of the radiators before being able to leave a room.

- Hovering at doorway thresholds, seemingly 'stuck' and unable to move through.

Strengths and skills

While children with ASD have many of the difficulties described, they may also have numerous strengths, skills and differences that are interesting or helpful. People with ASD tend to be logical and methodical. They may also be good with numbers and computers. Some people with ASD like certain types of art or music and may be interested in Japanese, Egyptian or historical cultures from the past. They can also be good at science, art or animation. People with ASD tend to like rules, fairness and honesty. All of these things may be great assets to them in life.

Preoccupations in children with ASD may be helpful to them in some situations. They may reduce anxiety or help children pursue their interests. It is important to remember that our aim in helping children with preoccupations may be to make sure preoccupations do not intrude into their lives excessively (e.g. their learning or relaxation). Detailed practical examples and strategies for parents and professionals are covered in Williams and Wright (2004).

2

WHAT IS A SOCIAL STORY?

Many professionals use the term 'social story' in different ways. Many parents may use off-the-shelf stories about everyday life to prepare children for certain experiences. They are stories with social information. This might include stories about going to the dentist, or a funeral or playing in the park.

The term Social Story describes something more specific. Social Stories were designed by Carol Gray and have been subject to years of thought, design and research. In this guide, whenever the word Story is capitalised it refers to a Social Story as defined by Carol Gray (see Part 2 for further information).

> *A Social Story accurately describes a context, skill, achievement or concept according to ten defining criteria. These criteria guide Story research, development and implementation to ensure an overall patient and supportive quality, and a format, 'voice', content and learning experience that is descriptive, meaningful, and physically, socially and emotionally safe for the child, adolescent or adult with autism. The criteria define what a Social Story is, and the process that researches, writes and illustrates it. (Gray 2015)*

What makes a Social Story different?

A Social Story follows certain 'rules'. These rules are very simple and designed to make sure that the Social Story is a positive experience for the child or young person. Another way of looking at this is that they are a checklist for making sure that your Social Story has a good chance of being helpful and nurturing to the young person and that it is safe to use in terms of the social information or advice it gives, and the way material is presented.

When should I write a Social Story?

It may be an anxious child or an unexpected behaviour from them that prompts teachers or parents to think about writing a Social Story. In the case of children with autism or Asperger syndrome, it is frequently because they have misunderstood a social situation. Social Stories can 'fill in the gaps' and share social information.

The difficulty children with autism have with requests and social situations may also extend to understanding praise. Praise from parents and professionals is often a general, short statement, as in 'Well done!' or 'Good work!' A child with autism may need more detail in order to know exactly what is being praised. Praise contributes to confidence and self-esteem, essential for all children. A Social Story may add detail and meaning to praise.

When you think the behaviour you see in a child with ASD is likely to be associated with a social misunderstanding and it is causing distress to them or others, it is worth considering writing a Social Story. The Social Story tries to improve the social understanding of the situation and context for the child. Even though this is not the main aim, the result of the Social Story is often a positive change in the child's behaviour. Similarly, when you notice that a new concept or skill has been mastered, or there's an opportunity to praise a child for an achievement, positive skill or a kindness, a Social Story helps to build detail and meaning into your comments.

What are they for?

They can help in situations which the child/young person finds distressing, frustrating and incomprehensible, or which appear to result in the child responding in a way that leads to more difficulties. They can help in situations where the child needs to understand praise. Some examples for what a Social Story can be used for are included in the following diagram. The table below refers to Stories in this guide which relate to the type of Story in the diagram.

What can a Social Story be used for?	Example Stories	Page
Preparation for transitions, change or new experiences	Joining school swimming lessons	95
	Finding out about Archbishop Holgate Sixth Form	102
	What happens when I have a seizure?	79
	Going to Flamingo Land	113
Praise, recognising, reinforcing, self-esteem	I am a kind, intelligent person	115
Information about life skills	Trying hard at swimming	92
	Focusing and concentrating	90
	Working on my own	88
	Taking new medicine	100
Information for keeping safe	Trying hard at swimming	92
	Spiderman is a film character	117
Understanding routines: School	Why we do homework	107
	Waiting to ask the teacher a question	111
	Taking turns to help in assembly	58
	Why we go to school	85
Understanding emotions and how to manage them	Happy playtimes	97
Understanding social behaviour or social communication	Using words that people like	119
	Happy playtimes	97
Giving reassuring information	Visiting the dentist	105
	How to take tests	109

Understanding people:
  Other people
  Myself
  Other people understanding me
	Why do we fart?	68

	Time to think	73

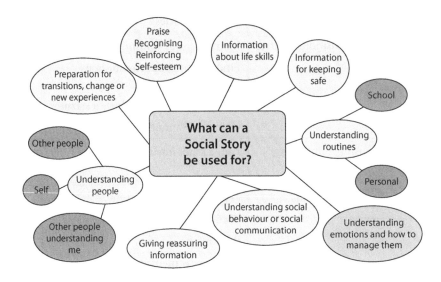

What is different about children with ASD? Why are Social Stories important for them?

The behaviour of children with ASD often makes them stand out as being different from their peers. For example, they might become very distressed in a new situation, push to the front of a queue, run around in a classroom when everyone else is sitting quietly or scream loudly and cover their ears if they hear certain sounds. There are many different examples every day for different children. These behaviours often occur for lots of reasons, including:

- being frightened in social situations

- not realising that other people are following social rules and not knowing what they are

- being distressed by something sensory (e.g. a noise like a hand dryer, or a perfume)

- not appreciating that other people have needs that are different to their own (see the section on mindblindness in Chapter 1)

- not 'getting the gist' of events such as a birthday party (see the section 'Getting the gist' in Chapter 1)

- an intense interest or preoccupation

- not being able to do what they want and/or not understanding, for example, that 'no' may really mean 'maybe later'

- difficulty with communication breakdown.

Children with ASD find it more difficult to understand the social world *intuitively* in the way that those without ASD do (this has been described in more detail in the previous chapter, 'Understanding Autism'). A situation may need to be broken down into steps with an explanation about social behaviour. We believe that Social Stories help children with ASD because:

- They are written for the child/young person and tailored to his or her ability and interests.

- They are written by the people who know the child best who can make the best guess as to what the child is struggling with and what information they need.

- All are written with positive phrasing, often celebrating the child's skills and successes.

- They are often reviewed several times whilst the child is learning a new skill to reinforce the message.

- The reading of the Story is a pleasant experience for the child because it is delivered in a positive context. Sometimes children read them independently.

- Sometimes the child can help writing them, which may highlight some issues with the Story as it is being written and allow the child to identify with it.

- They may enable a child to step back and to plan what to do in advance.

- They *give information* the child or young person did not have before.

- They often *reduce the anxiety* of the child.

- They attempt to address the problems associated with *mind-blindness* by giving children or young people some perspective on the thoughts, emotions and behaviours of others.

- They attempt to address *context blindness* by providing young people with information about the context in social situations to help them gain access to all the information that we assume 'everyone knows' (Vermeulen 2012).

- They encourage *understanding from others*.

- They help the individual *better predict* the actions and assumptions of others.

- They present information on social situations in a *structured and consistent* manner.

- The written word and/or pictures are more *permanent* than the spoken word so they can remember better.

- They provide a little *distance* between teaching and the possible stresses of the social situation itself.

- They give the child a chance to practise the skills often and on his or her terms.

- They often lead to an indirect positive change in social behaviour that has benefits for the child or young person.

- They allow the child to 'think through' (and imagine) the situation.

Part 2

A Guide to Writing
SOCIAL STORIES
for Teachers and Parents

3

A GUIDE TO SOCIAL STORIES

A summary of how to write a Social Story

This section breaks down and explains the process of writing Social Stories. It gives a structure around where and how to begin, continue and conclude.

There are *ten essential criteria*. The criteria give clear guidance on the elements that make a Social Story what it is. They lead a Social Story to be developed and delivered in a certain way, and have a particular definable set of characteristics that are thought to be important in their success. They are defined by Carol Gray, who designed Social Stories.

Although the plan to write a Social Story is sometimes triggered by a concern from parents or teachers about a young person's distress or anxiety, it is important to try to remember that half of all Social Stories written for an individual child applaud accomplished skills or praise achievements. It is extremely valuable to have parents' involvement throughout the process of developing a Social Story. They know their children best and can provide important information and support. Similarly, when parents are writing the Story, involvement from teachers and other adults who know the child often increases understanding, adds an additional perspective and ensures that the Story is tailored to the child. It will help greatly if the author(s) of the Story take some time to learn about autism and understand the perception of pupils with ASD. Children with autism perceive the world differently and hence their responses have to be understood within this context. One parent said that it helped her if she kept reminding herself to '*think autism*' whenever she recognised that her daughter was struggling with something (see Chapter 1). By this she meant that she should consider whether her daughter was unable to fully understand the context (get the gist) and/or the thoughts and feelings of others (mindblindness).

The following criteria go through the process of writing a Social Story in a stepwise logical fashion. They introduce the ten criteria and take you through what they mean in practice. At the end of this guide they are presented again in a long and short checklist form. The next section describes the process and also gives an example of going through the process of putting a Social Story together.

1. The 1st Criterion: The Goal

The Goal of a Social Story is to share accurate information using a format, voice, and content that is descriptive, meaningful, and physically, socially and emotionally safe for the Audience. (Gray 2015)

Remember that the overall Goal of a Social Story is to share accurate, socially meaningful information in a positive and reassuring way. It is not to change behaviour. However, the increased understanding they provide often results in positive change.

There may be occasions when you can borrow a Social Story which has already been written and adapt it a little to suit the topic and the child. These are really helpful (see, for example, Gray 2010, 2015; Gray and Leigh White 2001). However, because social situations are so wide and varied the majority of Social Stories are developed and written specifically for the child or young person for the particular situation. This guide was developed to help with the process of constructing Stories.

The example below shows the process of the construction of a Social Story for a child named Jodie following each of the criteria.

EXAMPLE: WRITING JODIE'S STORY

Jodie, aged 6 years, has Asperger syndrome. She was finding school assemblies very difficult and as part of a previous plan to help her to cope with them, she was frequently asked to help the teacher in assembly. However, when other children were asked to help she became very upset, often shouting loudly, hitting others, stamping her foot and crying. She had to be removed from the assembly hall and often took an hour or more to become calm. This was causing great distress to Jodie, the other children and teachers. Her teachers did not want to stop her from going to assembly, having made good progress previously, but realised that they could not continue as they were. They decided to consider a Social Story.

1. The Goal

Jodie's teachers were alerted to the fact that there was a problem for her in assembly by her behaviour. They realised that it was likely that she did not understand some aspect of the context and decided to try to discover exactly what the difficulty was from her perspective. It was her difficulty understanding the social situation that prompted them to consider a Social Story. Jodie's teachers explained the situation to her parents. They all agreed that a Social Story was the best way forward. By giving her social information about assembly within the positive framework of Social Stories, they believed that she could be gently guided to make sense of the situation and develop an understanding about what people usually do in assembly and why.

2. The 2nd Criterion: Two-Step Discovery

Keeping the Goal in mind, Authors gather relevant information to 1) improve their understanding of the Audience in relation to a situation, skill, or concept and/or 2) identify the specific topic(s) and type(s) of information to share in the Story. (Gray 2015)

i. Gather information to understand the specific situation the child is struggling with from their point of view.

ii. Then decide on the topic the child needs help with, and what information they need to be given to understand the situation better.

Gathering information is an essential, non-negotiable part of developing a Social Story. It is the process by which the child and their needs are better understood. For example, 'Why is the child frustrated? or 'What is it they do not understand?' Improvement in the child's self-esteem or behaviour often occurs as a result of improved understanding based on the information gained from this process. This guide follows Carol

Gray's newly revised 10.2 criteria, which are described in more detail in her book (Gray 2015).

2 i. Gathering information

- It is essential to talk to the people who know the child or young person best (e.g. parents, carers, teachers and the young person themselves when appropriate). They will be a great source of information. Think about the area of concern and why it might be a problem for the child. Take some time to generate and answer questions about what information is required for this particular child or young person for this particular issue. Ask questions related to the topic which begin with who, what, where, when, why and how.

- Observe the child in the situation. Consider what is happening from your perspective as an onlooker and then from the perspective of the child. Sometimes it can be helpful to record information, e.g. what was happening just before the child became upset?

- Remember to 'think autism'. Try to think about the ways in which autism affects the child in this situation. Does mindblindness mean that he cannot understand other people's points of view? Does her difficulty getting the gist prevent her from intuitively knowing about social expectations and the norms of social behaviour within the context of a school assembly? See Chapter 1 on understanding autism.

Chapter 4 contains further details on gathering information. It includes worked examples of using a template to help you to explore why a child with autism or Asperger syndrome might be struggling with a situation. A blank version of this template is also provided in the Appendices. When using the template, it helps if the person or people writing the Story consider the problem from the young person's point of view. With young people, it is often helpful to include them in this process.

2. Two-Step Discovery

2 i. Gathering information

Jodie's teachers observed her behaviour many times in assemblies and felt the trigger for her distress was other children being asked to help in assembly. However, they wanted to try to find out why she was struggling so badly when other children were chosen to help. They spoke to her parents and decided to complete the template in the Appendices together. They realised that due to her Asperger syndrome she had mindblindness. She had little or no understanding of the feelings of the other children or the fact that they might want a turn. All she knew was that she wasn't getting her turn and this made her very cross and distressed. Also, she still hadn't grasped the concept of the unwritten rules around expected behaviour in assemblies. She didn't 'get the gist' that people were expected to sit quietly in assembly. Again, this was related to her Asperger syndrome. She may also have become stuck in a routine around her expectation that she would always be the helper in assembly. In her mind and memory this was part of what assembly was for her.

By considering other aspects in the template, they realised that they had inadvertently contributed to the misunderstanding. They had built an expectation for her that she would be asked to help but had failed to explain that other children would be helping sometimes too. From her point of view, other children were taking her job, which made her feel very cross. They realised that she needed help to understand about taking turns and recognising others' perspectives. This was an ideal situation for writing a Social Story as it would enable her parents and teachers to help fill the gaps in Jodie's social understanding.

2 ii. Deciding on the topic

The gathering information stage often helps to provide the Story's focus or topic. The following is an example of this.

One boy, Joseph, refused to wear long trousers even in the winter months. His parents and teachers tried various different explanations to try to encourage him to wear long trousers in cold weather without success. It was only after a great deal of exploration that they realised he had become stuck in his thinking about his need to wear short trousers all of the time 'like the Victorian boys'. This understanding led them to be able to help him to move on. His parents wrote a Social Story for him about the differences in Victorian fashion for boys' trousers and modern fashion. They had discovered where the problem lay from their son's perspective. This gave them the topic for the Story 'Why boys in the Victorian era wore short trousers', and the opportunity to explain the context.

Try to keep the topic very specific and practical.

Gathering information helps to bring a Story down to a practical size. Sometimes we start with very big issues and problems that are too big to tackle and need more focus. For example, the issue that 'transitions seem difficult'. Gathering information may reveal the main problem is with waiting in a queue. The specific focus may then be 'Learning about waiting in queues at school'.

N.B. Decide if a Social Story is the best intervention. Sometimes, after the information is gathered, an alternative solution becomes apparent. For example, a teacher had wanted to develop a Social Story for a 7-year-old girl who appeared to be ignoring most of his instructions. Her expressive language was extremely good and the teacher had assumed that her verbal understanding was also good. In fact, when gathering information, it became clear that it was very poor. She did not understand his instructions and had developed a habit of 'switching off' when he spoke to her. In this case, a Social Story was not required. The intervention was for adults to reduce their language to short simple sentences. It may also become apparent that other interventions would be helpful before a Social Story is used, such as the use of a visual time table or other visual support systems.

Social Stories are a journey of exploration with the young person, and those supporting the young person can learn a lot from developing the Social Story. This is why gathering information is important.

EXAMPLE: WRITING JODIE'S STORY (CONT.)

2 ii. Deciding on the topic

The gathering information stage helped Jodie's teachers to decide on the topic 'Taking turns to help in assembly', which made the process of writing the Story much easier. They were quickly able to identify the social information they could share with Jodie to help her to understand why we take turns and to learn a little about others' perspectives.

3. The 3rd Criterion: Three Parts and a Title

A Social Story has a title and introduction that clearly identifies the topic, a body that adds detail, and a conclusion that reinforces and summarizes the information. (Gray 2015)

A Social Story has a good title, and three parts: a beginning (introduction), middle (body) and end (conclusion). A good title is clear to the child and is easy to understand. It describes what the Story is about. Don't forget, you can use a 'wh' question as the title for the Story (e.g. 'Where do I go at lunchtime?'). These can work especially well with young children.

    i. *Establish the focus and title of the Story.* Use the information from the 'gathering information' section to help you be clear about the focus of the Story and decide on a title based on this. Make it positive, simple and clear. Think about how to make it interesting to engage the child. Focus on understanding the things the child can do (or try to do), rather than on what they cannot do. Many Social Stories celebrate success.

    ii. *Introduction.* This introduces the Story and topic in a positive way. For example, 'I have many books about the Victorian era.' It is also an opportunity to applaud skills and positive attributes: 'My teacher says that I am very knowledgeable about history.'

    iii. *Body.* This is the main part of the Story. It is the section that gives a Story relevant detail and makes it interesting. Sometimes helpful information is obtained from the internet or books. For example, 'Boys in the Victorian era used to wear short trousers most of the time.' It also provides information about the relevant social cues, perspectives and common responses. 'That was the clothing fashion then. Fashion is a word used to describe the style of clothes that is popular at the time. In the Victorian era wealthy boys my age stayed indoors so they didn't need long trousers to keep warm. In 2015 it is the fashion for boys to wear long trousers in the winter months. This also helps us to keep warm. I will wear long trousers in winter because it is the fashion in 2015.' Remember that your main goal is not to change behaviour. It is to positively empower the child with information that is currently not available to them. The Goal of the Social Story is to share accurate social information.

iv. *Conclusion.* This summarises the message. End it on a positive note. 'It's a good idea to wear long trousers because it is the fashion in 2015 and my legs will stay warm!'

EXAMPLE: WRITING JODIE'S STORY (CONT.)

3. Three Parts and a Title

3 i. The focus and title

Having discovered that Jodie's misunderstanding was about taking turns, they titled the Story 'Taking turns to help in assembly'.

3 ii. Introduction

This Story starts by introducing the main people in the Story. First is Jodie, then her teacher. This describes some positive things about Jodie such as her favourite activity, Lego. It sets the scene, that is, where the event is focused – St Anselm's school. It introduces her teacher, Mrs Jessop: 'Mrs Jessop is usually my teacher.' The word 'usually' is important because all Stories need to be factually correct. Mrs Jessop might be busy or ill sometimes and a substitute teacher may have to take her place. Without the word 'usually', the Story isn't factually correct. Children with ASD are often very literal in their thinking. Jodie may become upset when a new teacher takes Mrs Jessop's place if she thinks Mrs Jessop will always be her teacher.

3 iii. The body of the Story

The body of Jodie's Story addresses the topic of her Story, 'Taking turns to help in assembly'. It aims to help her to understand that teachers choose children to help in assembly and that children take turns. It points out why she may not be chosen and what she might do if she isn't chosen. When writing this section of Social Stories, it is often really helpful to ask yourself 'wh' questions. Who does what, where, when and why. The answers to these questions will help guide you in forming this section. (See the 6th Criterion for more information about 'wh' questions.)

3 iv. The conclusion of the Story

The conclusion of the Story, 'The next assembly helper may be me or someone else. Either way, it is fair and okay,' is a reminder about the content of the Story and is very positive.

4. The 4th Criterion: FOURmat Makes it Mine!

The Social Story format is tailored to the individual's ability, attention span, learning style and, whenever possible, talents and interests of its Audience. (Gray 2015)

Write the text and use illustrations consistent with the child's ability.

This Criterion is about tailoring the Social Story to the child. This includes:

i. *Learning style.* Adapt the presentation of the Story to the child's learning style. Take into account their autism. All children are different. Some children learn more readily through pictures, others through the written word and others with both. Some may need to use just a few words with photos. Using rhythm, rhyme, song or repetition can be helpful. If the child is older or interested in facts, a chart may work well. Alternatively, if they learn best with computers, writing the Story on PowerPoint, which allows you to insert sounds or animation, may be helpful. Making a DVD may be useful for others. Tailor it to the specific individual.

ii. *Attention span.* Keep the Story as short as possible for children with a short attention span.

iii. *Level of understanding.* Check with the people who know the child best that the language or pictures used in the Story are within their comprehension level based on their age, and also their social and learning developmental level.

iv. *Language and reading ability.* Use language at the appropriate reading age for the child. For example, young children with autism may prefer Stories that contain short sentences and simple vocabulary, with large text. Children with limited language may learn best with lots of pictures. Older children may prefer Stories (or Social Articles) that contain more advanced vocabulary with accompanying graphs and charts.

If the Story reflects the child's interests and they can take ownership of it, this helps maximise success. The Story is written with knowledge of the child's personal interests and preferences in an effort to make Stories more interesting and/or fun to read. It increases the likelihood that the child will 'take ownership' of the material.

EXAMPLE: WRITING JODIE'S STORY (CONT.)

4. FOURmat Makes it Mine!

4 i. Learning style

Jodie usually learns well through the written word but she also enjoys pictures to illustrate her Stories. She loves clip art and symbols so she helped to illustrate the Story with her teaching assistant. She likes having a book about every Story and enjoys helping with the laminating and ring binding.

4 ii. Attention span

Jodie's Story was checked by her teachers and parents and was well within her attention span.

4 iii. Level of understanding

Her teaching assistant who knows Jodie very well ensured that the Story was written at the correct level for her.

4 iv. Language and reading ability

Jodie is a very able girl and can read very well.

5. The 5th Criterion: Five Factors Define Voice and Vocabulary

A Social Story has a patient and supportive voice that is defined by five factors. They are:

1. First and/or third person perspective;

2. Positive and patient tone;

3. Consideration of past, present, or future tense;

4. Literal accuracy;

5. Accurate vocabulary.

(Gray 2015)

This recognises the importance of the use of language and how the Story is told. Above all, the tone is positive and the information is accurate.

Social Stories are also an opportunity to enhance a child's self-esteem. The Story has a helpful and positive tone and the following five factors help to achieve this.

i. *Write sentences in the first (I, we) and/or third person (she, it, they).* 'You' statements can make the Story too directive and generally are not used. Where it is necessary to explain negative behaviours the third person is used. For example, use a 'learning vantage point' such as: 'Sometimes children may speak whilst someone else is still talking. This is called interrupting. With practice children learn when to talk and when to listen.'

ii. *The Story has a positive and patient tone.* This means being positive, non-judgemental and non-authoritarian. It also gives information to children about what they can try to do. An example of a negative sentence would be: 'I should not shout out in class'. Changing this into a positive sentence would be: 'Children try to put up their hands in class when they want to speak and then wait until the teacher asks them what they want to say.' The following is a list of potentially distressing words and phrases which we avoid in Social Stories (there are many others):

» should/shouldn't

» supposed to/mustn't

» ought/ought to know better

» bad/naughty

» never/always

» can't/don't.

iii. *Information from the past, present or future can be used in Social Stories.* Past information can be useful in building self-esteem, reminding people about previous positive events and outcomes and demonstrating the connection between the Audience's life experiences.

iv. *Social Stories are literally accurate.* Check that each word, phrase or sentence can be interpreted literally without changing the intended meaning. Children with autism may not understand complex, metaphorical phrases or words (e.g. 'pull your socks up') or phrases that might be understood in more than one way (e.g. 'take your seats'). However, occasionally, if a child understands and likes to use a known phrase it is fine to use metaphors. For example, one girl loved the phrase 'I am a star!' She used this phrase to mean that she was performing particularly well and used it to congratulate herself.

v. *Accurate meaning.* Be accurate in meaning, especially when using verbs. For example, Jane's teacher might say, 'Jane, could you take the register to Mr Jones in the office now please?' The word 'could' is not clear in meaning. It suggests that there is an option and invites the response of a simple 'Yes' or 'No'. The more direct request of 'Jane, take the register to Mr Jones in the office now please' is not open to misinterpretation.

EXAMPLE: WRITING JODIE'S STORY (CONT.)

5. Five Factors Define Voice and Vocabulary
5 i. Write sentences in the first and/or third person
All of the sentences in Jodie's Story are written in the first (I, we) and/or third person (she, it, they).

5 ii. A positive and patient tone
It has a positive and patient tone. It only uses positive language, mentioning what children can try to do rather than telling them what to do. 'When another child is chosen, I will try to sit quietly.' 'It is good to let the other children have a turn to help.'

5 iii. Information from the past, present or future

Many of the sentences in this Story refer to the past, present and future, for example 'Sometimes children are chosen to help in assembly.' Other sentences use the future tense, for example 'Mrs Jessop will be very happy if I try to sit quietly ' refers to something that may happen in the future. The mix of past, present and future tenses connect previous, present and future experiences.

5 iv. Literally accurate

Every statement is literally accurate. Whenever there is a possibility that the sentence may not be true at all times, this is qualified by the addition of words such as 'sometimes' or 'usually', for example 'Mrs Jessop is usually my teacher.' This allows for times when Mrs Jessop is not there (e.g. when she is ill or on a training course).

5 v. Accurate meaning

Reading through the Story carefully, it seems accurate and there are no obvious different interpretations which could be made.

6. The 6th Criterion: Six Questions Guide Story Development

A Social Story answers relevant "'wh" questions', describing the context (WHERE); time-related information (WHEN); relevant people (WHO); important cues (WHAT); basic activities, behaviors, or statements (HOW); and the reasons or rationale behind them (WHY). (Gray 2015)

This means the Social Story will often *answer* questions like who, what, when, why, where and how questions. You can also use these questions to explore the issues as you develop a Social Story.

Be inquisitive on behalf of the child. When you are aware what social information is missing, the Social Story can be designed to provide it. For example, a Story about 'Where is my class going?' would focus on the answers to the questions where, when, who and how.

The questions are also a great way to explore the gaps in information for the child as you develop the Story. Where and when does the issue occur?

Who does it involve? What are the gaps in the child's understanding? The child may need explanations for certain social conventions. They may need to understand what others need (e.g. dogs like to eat food). Answer the questions within the Story.

Ethan would not go into the classroom at wintertime. We asked some simple 'wh' questions like, 'Why does he not go into the classroom?' 'Why does he look frightened?' 'When did it start?' 'What has changed in the classroom?' His mum gave us the answers when she explained that it started at Christmas time when he became very frightened of tinsel. We discovered that there was a lot of tinsel in the classroom and he did not like it on his hands. This helped us write a Social Story that answered some 'wh' questions for him, like 'What is tinsel for?'

EXAMPLE: WRITING JODIE'S STORY (CONT.)

6. Six Questions Guide Story Development

Jodie's teacher considered asking questions like:

- What information does Jodie require to help her to understand about taking turns in assembly?
- Could we explain how we decide whose turn it is to help in assembly?
- Why is it important to take turns?
- What do we try to do when someone else is chosen?

7. The 7th Criterion: Seven is About Sentences

A Social Story is comprised of Descriptive Sentences and may have one or more Coaching Sentence. Sentences adhere to all applicable Social Story criteria. (Gray 2015)

Carol Gray found that Social Stories were much more successful when great care was taken about the use of words and sentences. The sentence types she describes are those which focus on the needs of children with autism. In many respects they are ordinary, everyday sentences; however, all ten of the Social Stories criteria are used together to ensure the positivity, care and respect required to produce a genuine Social Story with a high likelihood of success. Each of the sentence types has a different job in a Social Story. The names and descriptions given to them remind us of the gaps in the social understanding of children with autism. It is these gaps which we are trying to fill when writing the Stories.

In her book *The New Social Story Book, Revised and Expanded 15th Anniversary Edition* (2015), Carol Gray simplified the sentence Criterion by reducing the number of sentence types to two: Descriptive Sentences and Coaching Sentences. These are described below. Descriptive Sentences are the only essential Sentence types in Social Stories. Coaching Sentences are usually used but not a requirement. The different types are included as a guide to help with the writing process.

7 i. Descriptive Sentences

Descriptive Sentences accurately describe relevant aspects of context, including external and/or internal factors while adhering to all applicable Social Story criteria. They are free of assumption, bias, judgement, devaluation and/or unidentified opinion. (Gray 2015)

There are three main types of Descriptive Sentences. Those which:

1. describe observable external factors, including the situation and context

2. describe other peoples' internal states (e.g. thoughts and feelings)

3. enhance or reinforce the meaning of surrounding sentences.

Descriptive Sentences to describe observable external factors

Descriptive Sentences describe observable external factors related to a topic, including those that are not readily apparent (relevant thoughts, feelings, cultural expectations, etc.). (Gray 2015)

These are sentences that describe the situation and context factually and objectively. Importantly, they give information that we often assume everybody knows. This is typically information that children with autism do not hold intuitively and so need additional help through Social Stories to understand. Children with ASD are very literal in their thinking.

They may not 'get the gist' of most situations (see 'Getting the gist', page 17). This means that they cannot easily pull together all of the different components of a situation into a coherent whole. They may not understand the meaning of social situations. Descriptive Sentences describe the facts related to a situation clearly and accurately.

It is useful to ask 'wh' questions (see the 6th Criterion, 'Six Questions Guide Story Development') when writing the Story for a young person. This helps us to consider factors related to the issue that are not readily obvious. For example, for the boy who didn't like tinsel, his teachers asked themselves the question, 'Why do we use tinsel?' and 'What is tinsel?' They then included the answers to these questions in the Social Story.

Descriptive Sentences are also used to add positive, honest information about the young people. This makes the Story more enjoyable for them and also provides the opportunity for praise.

Descriptive Sentences to describe other peoples' internal states

Descriptive Sentences often describe or refer to another person's internal state, including but not limited to knowledge, feelings, beliefs, opinions, motivation, health, illness, personality, etc. (Gray 2015)

Children with autism have difficulty understanding the thoughts and feelings of others. This has been described as 'Mindblindness' or difficulty making guesses about how others think or feel (see 'Mindblindness', page 15). Descriptive Sentences also state the perspective of other people. They are used to help young people with autism to learn that other people have their own thoughts and feelings. They explain what people might think in certain situations and that the way people think and feel affects what they do. They are particularly useful in helping children with autism to recognise that some people may think differently and also in giving information about how other people may feel in certain situations. An example of a Descriptive Sentence which describes other peoples' internal state is, 'Many people like to see tinsel on a Christmas tree.'

Descriptive Sentences to enhance or reinforce the meaning of surrounding Sentences

Descriptive Sentences may also be used to enhance the meaning of surrounding statements by describing commonly held beliefs, values or traditions within a given culture. (Gray 2015)

These are used to enhance the meaning of other types of sentences. They usually come immediately after other Descriptive Sentences or Coaching Sentences in order to reinforce a point. They may reinforce a point about safety or a positive statement: for example, the first Descriptive sentence here describes an observable fact. The second Sentence is used to reinforce the first. 'Children take turns going down the slide. This is very important.'

7 ii. Coaching Sentences

Coaching Sentences gently guide behaviour via descriptions of effective Team or Audience responses, or structured Audience Self Coaching, adhering to all other applicable Social Story criteria. (Gray 2015)

These are sentences that gently guide or coach behaviour or suggest a behaviour or a response for the child or young person. They often begin with 'I will try to...' or 'I may choose to...', or list the possibilities. They can also be used to guide the adults in the Story, for example 'Mrs Smith will try to give me more time to finish my spelling test.' Additionally, they can be useful for self-coaching (written by the young person themselves), for example 'To help me to stay calm at school, I will try to think about the next fun activity.'

There are three types of Coaching Sentences, which:

1. describe or suggest responses for the child, e.g. 'I may choose to work on a table where there is no tinsel'

2. describe or suggest responses for the caregiver, e.g. 'The teacher will try to set up some tables with tinsel and some tables without tinsel'

3. are developed by the child themselves (with the support of the caregiver), e.g. 'I may choose to play at the water table or with the trains (the child chooses)'.

7. Seven is About Sentences

7 i. Descriptive Sentences

The sentences in Jodie's Story are mostly *Descriptive* Sentences. They are statements of fact. They set the scene: 'My name is Jodie and I go to Saint Anselm's school.' They help children with ASD to learn the facts about a situation which they do not understand intuitively in the way that most typically developing children do (see Part 1). Jodie did not know that there was a process involved in teachers choosing children to help in assembly. She probably didn't realise that most of the time she wouldn't be chosen. It is unlikely that she knew that all of the children take turns. These Descriptive Sentences provide her with factual information. 'Sometimes children are chosen to help in assembly. Teachers decide who will be chosen to help. Sometimes I am chosen to help. Most of the time, someone else will be chosen.'

There is a Descriptive Sentence to explain her teacher's feelings and how they are affected by Jodie's actions: 'Mrs Jessop will be very happy if I try to sit quietly.' Another Descriptive Sentence reinforces the message about taking turns at the end of the Story: 'The next assembly helper may be me or someone else. Either way, it is fair and okay.'

7 ii. Coaching Sentences

There is only one Coaching Sentence. This is the one that coaches or gently guides Jodie about what she should try to do if she isn't chosen. 'When another child is chosen, I will try to sit quietly.' The word 'try' is important to add because it is unlikely that she will be successful all of the time and so the statement wouldn't be factually correct.

8. The 8th Criterion: A GR-EIGHT Formula!

A Formula that ensures that every Social Story describes more than directs. (Gray 2015)

This is to check the balance of sentences.

Carol Gray rightly explains that stories that tell children off or simply tell them what to do are not helpful and may lower a child's self-esteem. The point of a Social Story is to be constructive and helpful, to give the child information and help the child feel good about themselves. So we need to make sure the balance of sentences is right and this rule helps us do that. Descriptive Sentences describe the relevant facts, thoughts and feelings. Sentences that coach are more directive.

The simple formula below balances the use of sentences to ensure that every Social Story describes more than directs.

To keep this balance correct, add up all the Descriptive Sentences and divide that number by the number of Coaching Sentences. It can be called a Social Story if the answer is greater than or equal to 2.

EXAMPLE: WRITING JODIE'S STORY (CONT.)

8. A GR-EIGHT Formula!

There is only one Coaching Sentence in Jodie's Story and 11 other Directive Sentences. The sum to calculate the correct balance of sentences is therefore 11 divided by 1 = 11. The answer is greater than 2. So we easily have the correct balance.

9. The 9th Criterion: Nine to Refine

Every Social Story is Reviewed and Revised until it meets all applicable Social Story Criteria. (Gray 2015)

Editing the draft

When the Story has been written it is worth taking a few moments to use the helpful checklists (see checklists in the Appendices) and edit your first draft(s). This is *really* important. Checking that you have all of the ingredients and criteria in place will give you the best chance of success!

EXAMPLE: WRITING JODIE'S STORY (CONT.)

9. Nine to Refine

There were several drafts to this Story. It was checked by Jodie's parents and members of staff and the short checklist (see Appendices) was used several times to ensure that that all criteria were met.

10. The 10th Criterion: Ten Guides to Implementation

The Ten Guides to Implementation ensure that the philosophy and criteria that guide Story development are consistent with how it is introduced and reviewed with the Audience. (Gray 2015)

10 i. Plan for comprehension

Have a final check through the text to ensure that the information is clear and easy for the young person to understand.

10 ii. Plan Story support

You may want to add photographs, drawings or illustrations from the internet to make it more interesting for the child.

10 iii. Develop a Story schedule

Where will the Story be read? Find a quiet, comfortable place. Most young people prefer to have a private space away from their peers. Consider that Stories are often personal and private and this needs to be respected by adults. Some young people may want the Story to be confidential and may not want to be singled out from their class. When reading the Story, sitting next to the young person or slightly behind them may work best for younger children. Some older children may choose to read the Story on their own. It can be in the home and/or school setting. Find out what the child would prefer or what would be most helpful to them. It can also be a combination of places.

When and *how* often will the Story be read? Parents and teachers often know best when the best time to read a Social Story might be. This might be just before the event, or early in the day when the child is feeling most alert or possibly at a set time daily. It might be more than once a day, or once every few days. One child was unsure about the rules in a game of tig. His teacher read him the Story each morning for a few days in advance of the games lesson and then also, on the day of the event, she read it with him just a few minutes before it was due to start. Plan the most suitable times in advance. Many children love their Social Stories and ask to go back to them time and time again.

A Story is never used immediately after (or as a consequence of) misbehaviour.

10 iv. Plan a positive introduction

Think about *how* you would like to introduce the Story. Who will introduce the Story to the child and how? This works well if it is someone who knows and understands the child. Always introduce it in a positive manner. It often helps to begin with quiet confidence: 'This is that great Story we wrote together' or 'Do you remember when we talked about…'

10 v. Reading and monitoring the Story

Try to make sure that you are well prepared, feeling positive and calm and have time to introduce the Story to the child. Ensure that the child is ready to enjoy the Story and get something positive out of it. Listen to their comments and monitor their reactions, and be prepared to change anything that isn't quite right.

10 vi. Organise the Stories

Many children want to keep their Stories and refer back to them so it is worth making the Stories easy to access and storing them together in a safe place (e.g. a ring binder). They can form the basis for building concepts or understanding of the bigger picture for the child in the future.

10 vii. Mix and match Stories to build concepts

It is very common for numerous Stories to be generated around particular topics. They help to build concepts. It is useful to keep these filed together so that they can be revisited and reinforced.

10 viii. Story reruns and sequels

It is also useful to build on previous Stories.

10 ix. Recycle into applause

When a child has learned a new skill, the Story can be turned into a Story praising them for their achievement. This is a really easy and effective way of increasing the self-esteem of the child in the future.

10 x. Keeping the Story current

Monitor the Story periodically to keep it up to date.

10. Ten Guides to Implementation

10 i. Plan for comprehension

Jodie's teachers completed a final check for comprehension.

10 ii. Plan Story support

Jodie drew some pictures with her teacher to illustrate the Story, which they stuck into the small booklet they had made.

10 iii. Develop a Story schedule

Her teacher took some time to decide who would read the Story and how, when and where to present it.

10 iv. Plan a positive introduction

Her teaching assistant (whom Jodie knew well) read the Story. Jodie has some of her lessons in a small room next to her classroom. She likes reading books and her Social Story books are kept there because it is a quiet 'private' space.

10 v. Reading and monitoring the Story

The Story was read to her a few times in the small room over a period of 3 days to make sure that Jodie had a chance to ask any questions and alterations could be made accordingly. It was then read a few minutes before assembly was due to commence for 2 weeks.

10 vi. Organise the Stories

Jodie had several Stories written for her about assembly and already possessed a special folder marked 'Assemblies'. She chose to keep this Story with her previous ones and clearly enjoyed rereading them all.

TAKING TURNS TO HELP IN ASSEMBLY

My name is Jodie and I go to Saint Anselm's school. *(Descriptive)*

I love playing with Lego figures at free-play time. *(Descriptive)*

Mrs Jessop is usually my teacher. *(Descriptive)*

In school the children usually go to assemblies. *(Descriptive)*

Sometimes children are chosen to help in assembly. *(Descriptive)*

Teachers decide who will be chosen to help. *(Descriptive)*

Sometimes I am chosen to help. *(Descriptive)*

Most of the time, someone else will be chosen. *(Descriptive)*

When another child is chosen, I will try to sit quietly. *(Coaching)*

It is good to let the other children have a turn to help. *(Descriptive)*

We all have to take turns so that everyone gets a chance to help. *(Descriptive)*

Mrs Jessop will be very happy if I try to sit quietly. *(Descriptive)*

The next assembly helper may be me or someone else. Either way, it is fair and okay. *(Descriptive)*

Part 3

Gathering Information and
SOCIAL STORIES
Worked Examples

4

GATHERING INFORMATION

This section was included at the request of teachers and parents who wanted more detail, ideas and examples to help them with the process of gathering helpful information when they were unsure about why the young person was finding a particular situation or concept difficult. Gathering information is the process by which we develop a greater understanding of the child or young person and any difficulties they face. Armed with this understanding we are in a better position to target and provide the specific social information the child or young person needs. This makes writing a Social Story much easier. To help you do this we have provided a template in the Appendices and two examples on how to use these to gather information.

- *What* is the problem or the social situation you would like to help the young person with?

- *Why* does the child behave in this way at present?

- *What* does the child or young person need help with?

- *What* specifically do you hope the child will learn?

- *What* information would be helpful to the child?

- *Where* does it happen? What is the context?

TOP TIP: The *process* of trying to understand the child's perspective and needs is *really* important. This is the way you will discover what is really going on.

What is the problem or the social situation you would like to help the young person with?

Ask yourself what it is you are trying to help the young person with or what anxiety you are trying to reduce. The following are examples of behaviours that might prompt you to consider a Social Story.

- Amy became visibly worried when assembly was coming up.

- George kept on passing wind at school.

- Donald finds it difficult to take turns. He rolls the dice repeatedly and frequently interrupts others when playing games.

- Fred kept on telling people about his interests at length but wasn't listening to others.

- Sarah repeatedly became angry with her teacher when he tried to help her in class.

Why does the child behave in this way?

This is especially helpful if you are trying to help the child to prepare for a difficult social situation (e.g. why do you think they will struggle with this?). You will usually need to improve your understanding of the situation as the first step in this process. This involves *gathering information*.

- Talk about the situation to the people who know the child well:

  » parents (always required)

  » others who know the child/young person well

  » the young person when appropriate.

- Observe the young person in the situation.

- Think about the problem from the young person's point of view. There is a blank template provided in the Appendices to help you with this process, and there are two completed examples for different situations later in this chapter.

TOP TIP: The person who is writing a Social Story with a child should always be someone who knows them well.

It is particularly important to consider the core difficulties associated with ASD for all children and young people with ASD, for example mindblindness and 'getting the gist'. Try to 'see' the situation from the perspective of a child with ASD. *Think autism.*

What does the child or young person need help with?

Now that you have a better understanding of *why* he or she is struggling or behaving in a certain way (e.g. anxiety) you can decide *what* he or she needs help with. This is often about a lack of understanding or misunderstanding of a social situation.

What specifically do you hope the child will learn?

Try to be clear about what you hope they will learn in order to check whether or not the Social Story has achieved what is needed for the child, including an increase in the social understanding of the situation. Try to be clear about what you are hoping will change. This may be a reduction in anxiety or learning a specific skill or a specific behaviour (e.g. seeking help by putting their hand up in class). In order to avoid too much complexity SMART objectives are sometimes helpful. SMART applies criteria that allow us to keep aims simple: any aims for positive support or change should be Specific, Measurable, Achievable, Realistic and Time limited (SMART).

- *Specific.* Try to be clear about your aim. Avoid being too general. Keep it clear and specific.

- *Measurable.* Most positive change can be measured in some way. It is helpful when the child, parents or teachers can identify the good new things happening and give praise. This is usually things that are happening more often (e.g. requesting help in class) but sometimes may be things happening less often (a child having fewer episodes of intense distress).

- *Achievable.* Can this be achieved or have you set your expectations too high?

- *Realistic.* Is the aim realistic for the young person?

- *Time limited.* Set a time when you will review and monitor things. It is common to need to adjust a Social Story or set your sights on a more modest aim.

What information would be helpful to the child?

After gathering information about the child you are supporting it will often become clear what information the child is missing. Think carefully about what this is and how you can provide it in a positive way. The template in the Appendices is designed to help with gathering information.

Worked example using the template (George)

This example is about what George does that his teachers would like to be different.

What is the problem?

George kept on passing wind (he called this farting) at school.

Why does the child behave in this way at present?

The shaded sections are to do with ASD.

Mindblindness Can they see others' points of view or understand feelings and needs of others in this situation? Do they realise they need to communicate their needs to someone?	*Due to his autism, he does not realise that the smell from him passing wind is unpleasant for his peers. His mindblindness prevents him from being able to consider their discomfort intuitively.*
Getting the gist Does the child understand the social meaning of the situation? Do they know what to expect and how to respond to this social situation? Do they need help with this?	*He does not get the gist about the social conventions around passing wind in public. He needs help with this, e.g. he needs to know that it is not polite and that there is something he can do to help, e.g. go to the toilet to pass wind. He also does not understand the cause of passing wind.*

Communication Do they understand the need to communicate, what to say and why? Do they need help to explain their actions, which may seem very reasonable to themselves?	*He may also need help in knowing what to say when he passes wind before he has chance to go the toilet, e.g. to say 'Excuse me'.*
Imagination Does the child think imaginatively? Does this affect their ability to play? Have they interpreted something literally? Is the problem to do with lack of ability to plan?	*He finds planning difficult and so benefits from clarity about what to do.*
Sensory experiences Is the problem associated with sensory experiences (the smell, sound, feel, taste, colour or look of something)? Are they frightened or in pain? Are their preoccupations interfering with learning?	*In this case the sensory experience for his peers was the main issue rather than his own sensory experience.*
Preoccupations and routine Is it to do with a need for routine or habits? Is there a need to be in control? Has there been a change of routine at home or at school?	*For George, farting in public had become a habit. Although people around him complained, saying, 'Oh George, you have farted again!' he was not concerned about this.*
Situations and settings Where does it happen? Where does it not happen? Who is around when it happens?	*George was in the habit of farting in most situations. The decision was made by his teachers and parents to work on the school situation initially.*
Triggers and timings When does it happen? What are the timings in relation to other things? When does it not happen? What is the trigger? Is it related to anxiety or the child's temperament? Is there anything that might be upsetting the child (e.g. memories, illness, tiredness, boredom)?	*No particular triggers were identified.*
Responses and reinforcers How have others responded? Does something happen after the behaviour that is important? How does it affect the behaviour in the future? What are the benefits of this behaviour? For you? For the child? (Rack your brains, there usually are some.)	*Sometimes, his peers laughed about George's passing wind in class. George may have thought that farting was a funny thing to do. He enjoyed their response and so in some ways this was reinforcing.*

What does the child or young person need help with?

Using the information gathered from others and from the template, the following became clearer.

George does not realise that the smell from him passing wind is unpleasant for his peers, he needs help to know that it is not polite and that there is something he can do to help (e.g. go to the toilet to pass wind), he needs help in understanding what causes wind and in knowing what to say when he passes wind before he has the chance to go the toilet (e.g. to say 'Excuse me'). In addition, it would be helpful for his teachers to ask his peers to simply walk away if George is passing wind in class rather than laughing if possible.

All of this information is really helpful for writing your Social Story. It contains the key components of the final Story for George. Importantly, the decision was made to present the Story largely in the third person. This gave those writing the Story the opportunity to present the physiological facts and the social information he required to understand about passing wind without focusing too much on him personally. Social Stories aim to remain positive about the individual and to preserve their self-esteem. This Story presents the facts George requires and only in the final paragraph refers to him as a reminder about what to do if he needs to fart. The final Story is presented below.

Most of the sentences in this Story are Descriptive Sentences. They describe facts or describe the context and social information, which we often assume everybody knows. There are two Coaching Sentences: 'If someone is feeling like they are going to fart, they try to go to the bathroom' and 'If I feel like I am going to fart in class or when I am at the dinner table, I will try to remember to ask to be excused and go to the bathroom.'

What specifically do you hope will change?

- *Specific.* In George's example, the behaviours his teachers and parents were hoping would increase were:

  » an increase in the number of times he left the room to go to the toilet to fart

  » an increase in the number of times he said 'Excuse me' when he farted in class

  » a decrease in the number of times he farted in class.

- *Measurable.* The teacher was able to congratulate George a number of times when he left the room to go to the toilet and also the times he apologised.

- *Achievable.* Do you believe it is 'do-able'? His parents and teachers thought so.

- *Realistic.* He had occasionally gone to the toilet before to pass wind and also said, 'Excuse me' so his parents and teachers knew that this was realistic.

- *Time limited.* It was agreed that parents and teachers would review things after 5 school days.

WHY DO WE FART?

Farts happen when we pass gas from our digestive system and out of our back passage. There are different names for farts. Some people call it flatulence or trumping or passing wind or passing gas. *(Descriptive)*

Farts are made of gas! All people fart sometimes during the day. It is normal. When we eat, we don't swallow just our food. We also swallow air, which contains gases like nitrogen and oxygen. Other gases like hydrogen, carbon dioxide (the gas that makes lemonade fizzy) and methane are made when food is digested in the large intestine. All of these gases in the digestive system have to escape somehow, so they come out as farts! *(Descriptive)*

Gases are also what can make farts smell bad. Many people don't like the smell of farts. *(Descriptive)* The smell makes them feel uncomfortable. *(Descriptive)* It is not polite to fart in social situations, like in class or at the dinner table. If someone is feeling like they are going to fart, they try to go to the bathroom. *(Coaching)* This is a good thing to do. *(Descriptive)* If a fart happens accidentally, it is important to remember to say 'Excuse me'!

Farting can sometimes be your body's sign that it's time to go to the toilet. If I feel like I am going to fart in class or when I am at the dinner table, I will try to remember to ask to be excused and go to the bathroom. *(Coaching)* This is the polite thing to do. *(Descriptive)*

Worked example using the template (Matthew)

This Story is a good example of the value of taking time to talk to the young person about a problem which is perceived very differently by themselves than by others.

What is the problem?

Matthew, aged 13 years, sometimes appears to 'shut down' and puts his head on the desk and covers his ears with his hands. This sometimes continues through a whole lesson. When his teachers offer him help he gets distressed and angry and feels very frustrated.

Why does the child behave in this way at present?

The shaded sections are to do with autism.

Mindblindness Can they see others' points of view or understand feelings and needs of others in this situation?	*Matthew finds it difficult to understand that his teachers think he needs help.*
Getting the gist Does the child understand the social meaning of the situation? Do they know what to expect and how to respond to this social situation? Do they need help with this?	*He doesn't know that when he puts his head down on his desk they think that this means he is finding the work too difficult.*
Communication Do they understand the need to communicate, what to say and why? Do they need help to explain their actions, which may be very plausible to themselves?	*He is unaware of the need to explain why he sometimes puts his head on the desk. To him, this is the best way to concentrate. His frustration and angry behaviour is sometimes caused by the interruptions of his well-meaning teachers.*
Imagination Does the child think imaginatively? Does this affect their ability to play? Have they interpreted something literally? Is the problem to do with lack of ability to plan?	*He sometimes finds it hard to plan which makes it difficult for him to complete his work. He lacks awareness of this but his current behaviour means that he isn't ready to accept help with it.*

Sensory experiences Is the problem associated with sensory experiences (the smell, sound, feel, taste, colour or look of something)? Are they frightened or in pain? Are their preoccupations interfering with learning?	*Matthew is very sensitive to noise and needs to attempt to shut out the distractions around him in class in order to concentrate. This is why he holds his hands over his ears.*
Preoccupations and routine Is it to do with a need for routine or habits? Is there a need to be in control? Has there been a change of routine at home or at school?	*He is trying to increase his independence.*
Situations and settings Where does it happen? Where does it not happen? Who is around when it happens?	*It happens when he is trying to concentrate in class.*
Triggers and timings When does it happen? What are the timings in relation to other things? When does it not happen? What is the trigger? Is it related to anxiety or the child's temperament? Is there anything that might be upsetting the child (e.g. memories, illness, tiredness, boredom)?	*The trigger for his angry and distressed behaviour is being asked if he needs help. He is determined to work independently whenever possible.*
Responses and reinforcers How have others responded? Does something happen after the behaviour that is important? How does it affect the behaviour in the future? What are the benefits of this behaviour? For you? For the child? (Rack your brains, there usually are some.)	*His teachers have tried to help him because they think he is stuck with his work when he puts his head down. Matthew gets angry with them and they feel frustrated because they think they are letting him down by not helping him. So they often keep trying which makes Matthew feel angrier. When his teachers were gathering information Matthew told them that he doesn't want help most of the time and that he puts his head down to help him to concentrate.*

What does the child or young person need help with?

The information gathered from the template his parents and teachers completed together gave them a greater understanding about his behaviour. His autism meant that he was unable to understand his teachers' perspective. He didn't know that they were trying to help him and became annoyed when they asked him if he needed help. After a long discussion with Matthew, it became clear that he needed to put his head on the desk in order to concentrate. He also needed some time to think and process things. The well-meaning offer of help by his teachers interrupted his thinking time, causing frustration. It was very important to him to try to complete the worksheets independently when possible.

Matthew, his teacher and parents wrote this Story together. It served the dual purpose of helping Matthew to understand his teachers a little better and helping his teachers to understand why he was becoming frustrated.

What specifically do you hope will change?

The hope was that Matthew's teachers would understand his need to have time to think and give him more time to think. Along with this Matthew would understand that his teachers were there to help. At this point Matthew was reluctant to accept a lot of help from teachers. It was anticipated that another Social Story might be written about this at a later date.

In order to avoid too much complexity SMART objectives are sometimes helpful. SMART applies criteria that allow us to keep aims simple: any aims for positive support or change should be Specific, Measurable, Achievable, Realistic and Time-limited (SMART).

- *Specific.* Clear and specific. That Matthew would be less frustrated and that his teachers would give him time to think.

- *Measurable.* Have an aim that you can measure. This was measured by (i) the number of times Matthew was able to stay calm in each lesson; (ii) the number of specific aggressive behaviours (e.g. shouting, throwing his chair); and (iii) the times his teachers interrupted him to ask if needed help.

- *Achievable.* This seemed achievable to Matthew and his teachers. Matthew wanted to work on his own and his teachers wanted to respect his wishes.

- *Realistic.* This specific aim felt realistic to Matthew and his teachers. His teachers remained a little concerned that he may continue to be stuck and not be able to produce his work without help but were very happy with the plan. They were aware that this may be the first of several Stories about this topic.

- *Time limited.* They decided to review progess after a 3-week period.

TIME TO THINK

Sometimes as part of my lesson I have to complete worksheets. *(Descriptive)*

Most of the time I do this successfully without help from my TA or teacher. *(Descriptive)*

Sometimes my TA or teacher may offer me extra help when I don't really need it. *(Descriptive)*

This is because I may look unsure but I am just concentrating and I need more time to process things. *(Descriptive)*

It is really difficult for my TA or teacher to know when I need extra help and when I can manage on my own. *(Descriptive)*

I prefer to do things on my own when I can, it makes me feel proud of myself and I learn better. *(Descriptive)*

Woohoo! *(Descriptive)*

Sometimes to help me concentrate I put my head down and cover my ears. *(Descriptive)*

My teachers will try to leave me alone when I do this. *(Coaching)*

Now they know that I need time to think. *(Descriptive)*

It's great to have time to think. *(Descriptive)*

Why we like this Story

This Story is a good example of the importance of gathering information carefully before writing. Matthew's teachers had felt stuck themselves because they were so keen to help Matthew and were frustrated with his rejection of their support. They had hoped that a Story about Matthew accepting their help would be the solution. Filling in the template helped them to realise that it was more complex than this. They realised that the additional information they discovered meant that listening to Matthew's perspective and respecting his wishes was essential. Matthew was very involved in writing the Story and was pleased with this final version. Gathering information often helps to focus on the young person's perspective and needs, and frequently changes the topic of the Story.

It is also a good example of the way in which some Stories and the process of writing them can help other people to understand the young person better. The Coaching Sentence in this Story is for the teachers.

TOP TIP: Remember to talk to the young person about the problem. Ensure that this is done in a gentle and exploratory, non-judgemental way.

Worked example without the template (Thomas)

Often, gathering information doesn't require the use of the template, although it can be used as a guide in facilitating the process. The example below is included to provide a summary of the criteria Thomas's mum followed when she was writing this Story.

What happens when I have a seizure?

Thomas started having epileptic seizures when he was 12 years old. He has delayed speech but his understanding is more developed. Before, during and after seizures, he looked very concerned and bewildered. His mum, Sarah, wanted to know how to help him to understand what was going on so that she could provide some reassurance during what could be a scary event.

The 1st Criterion: The Goal

Sarah arranged a meeting with the school staff to try to find a way to help Thomas. They had used Social Stories successfully in the past with Thomas and wondered about trying one for this situation. The Goal of a Social Story is to share accurate, meaningful information in a positive and reassuring way.

The 2nd Criterion: Two-Step Discovery

Thomas's teachers and parents shared information and decided on the topic for a Social Story. At the meeting, they discussed how having a seizure might feel for Thomas. They thought about what happened before, during and after a seizure and how scary this must be for him. They had observed his seizures several times and agreed that there was a consistent pattern. Although he was not able to communicate very much verbally, his behaviour showed that he knew something was wrong and that he felt unwell. They agreed that it would be helpful to give him information about what was happening when he had a seizure. Thomas was still under medical investigation to treat his epilepsy but it was taking some time to find the correct treatment for him. His teachers and parents realised that he still needed help and that a Social Story was the way forward.

They decided that he needed help to understand in simple terms what was happening and who might help.

The 3rd Criterion: Three Parts and a Title

i. *Establish the focus of the Story.* The Story was designed to explain what happened when Thomas had a seizure and so was called 'What happens when I have a seizure?'

ii. *Introduction.* It is introduced with a clear statement, 'My name is Thomas', which establishes immediately that it is about him. It then continues with positive factual statements, e.g. 'I like playing with Lego and cars.'

iii. *Body.* The middle part of the Story explains that Thomas has epilepsy and what this means: 'This means that I have seizures.'

It explains where they happen, what happens and how it feels when he has a seizure. It adds important reassuring facts so that he knows what other people will do, e.g. 'Adults will try to help to keep me safe.'

iv. *Conclusion.* It has a clear ending with reassurance that he will feel better when he wakes up from his sleep: 'I will be okay.'

The 4th Criterion: FOURmat Makes it Mine!

Tailor the Story and format to the child. Thomas's name is used at the beginning of the Story. It is about something relevant to him and it uses the first person (I) frequently.

i. *Learning style.* Thomas can understand simple language well. He likes short Social Stories to be written and to have simple coloured illustrations on the same page.

ii. *Attention span.* He prefers short Stories of less than 20 sentences.

iii. *Level of understanding.* His parents try to use the correct medical terminology where possible. They decided to use the words 'epilepsy' and 'seizures' as these were terms that he had heard frequently and now associated with the experience.

iv. *Language and reading ability.* Although Thomas cannot read, he likes to see the words on a page in book format with illustrations.

The 5th Criterion: Five Factors Define Voice and Vocabulary

i. All of the sentences relating to Thomas either use his name or the first (I, we) person.

ii. It has a positive and patient tone.

iii. It uses information from the past, present and future. It includes what happened before, during and after the seizure.

iv. Every statement is literally accurate. It is factually correct based on what they saw and what happened when he had a seizure. The words 'usually' and 'most of the time' are included in this Story. They are used when something may not happen all of the time. For example, 'I usually sleep after a seizure.' Thomas did usually fall asleep after a seizure but sometimes, particularly when he was trying a new medication, this did not happen. Similarly, although he appeared to feel better when he woke up after a seizure, very occasionally this was not true, so 'most of the time' was included in the sentence 'Most of the time I feel much better when I wake up.'

v. There are no obvious different interpretations that could be made by a young person with ASD.

The 6th Criterion: Six Questions Guide Story Development

Who, what, when, where, why and how questions have been asked to try to ensure that any gaps in Thomas's understanding of the situation have been considered.

The 7th Criterion: Seven is About Sentences

This Story contains mostly Descriptive Sentences or statements that are factual and describe what happens when he has a seizure. There is one Coaching Sentence: 'Adults will stay with me and keep me safe.' (Coaching Sentences gently guide the behaviour of young person or the adults who are trying to help them; in this case, it is gently guiding the adults – it identifies what the adults will do to help Thomas.)

The 8th Criterion: A GR-EIGHT Formula!

There is only one Coaching Sentence in Thomas's Story and 18 Directive Sentences. The sum to calculate the correct balance of sentences is therefore 18 divided by 1 = 18. The answer is greater than 2. So the Story has the correct balance. This is important because it helps to maintain positivity and reassurance and avoids a tone of telling the child what to do. The focus is on describing the situation.

The 9th Criterion: Nine to Refine

The Story focuses on Thomas. It was written for him with all the criteria in mind. His family and teachers used the checklist in the Appendices to ensure that they were following the criteria. They made several changes and edited it as required.

The 10th Criterion: Ten Guides to Implementation

They read the Story with him to check his understanding.

Sarah decided to use the Story at home initially, in a quiet room where they like to spend time together. As there was no way of predicting his seizures, she chose to read the Story on a regular but infrequent basis. He didn't really like to look at it at first but didn't push it away and seemed interested in the pictures.

After reading the Story a few times Thomas liked his mum to say, 'I will be okay' when they read it together. He smiled and turned his thumbs upwards to mean 'okay'. It seemed that he gained some reassurance from reading the Story, which was the original intention.

WHAT HAPPENS WHEN I HAVE A SEIZURE? (THOMAS'S STORY)

My name is Thomas. *(Descriptive)*

I like playing with Lego and cars. *(Descriptive)*

I love going to the Railway Museum. *(Descriptive)*

I have epilepsy. *(Descriptive)*

This means that I have seizures. *(Descriptive)*

Seizures make me go quiet and still. *(Descriptive)*

They make me feel a bit wobbly. *(Descriptive)*

Sometimes I feel sick before a seizure. *(Descriptive)* This is okay. *(Descriptive)*

It is a warning that a seizure is going to happen next. *(Descriptive)*

When this happens Mum usually says, 'It's okay. It is just a seizure.'

Seizures can happen at school or at home or when I am outside. *(Descriptive)*

If I am at home or outside when I have a seizure, my mum or dad will stay with me. *(Descriptive)*

If I am at school when I have a seizure, one of my teachers will stay with me. *(Descriptive)*

Adults will stay with me and keep me safe. *(Coaching)*

My seizures are usually finished in about 2 minutes. *(Descriptive)*

I usually sleep after the seizure. *(Descriptive)*

Most of the time I feel much better when I wake up. *(Descriptive)*

I can go and play with my Lego and cars! *(Descriptive)*

I will be okay. *(Descriptive)*

Why we like this Story

Thomas's communication difficulties made it hard for him to make sense of his seizures. The Story was written to help him to understand them a little better and to offer him reassurance that there was a plan in place to support him when he was having a seizure. His parents were unsure how much he would understand but felt that he found it helpful as a way of giving him a consistent message that he would be okay. It showed them that he was able to understand more than he could say. He used his thumbs-up sign at the end of his Story and eventually after his seizure had finished. This was his first Social Story and it motivated his parents to write more in the future.

When not to use Social Stories

Social Stories can help with many situations but don't forget to consider other options instead of or as well as the Stories. Other support or interventions may be appropriate. For example, consider:

- *Visual time tables.* This is where a series of pictures can be used to explain a sequence of future events. This might be individual pictures showing the planned activities for the school day in the order in which they will occur, e.g. assembly, reading, playtime, etc. These time tables and first/then (see below) cards help to spread less popular activities between more popular ones. They also help reduce anxiety, motivate children to do things that are helpful to them and encourage independence. See *How to Live with Autism and Asperger Syndrome* and *Intervention and Support for Parents and Carers of Children and Young People on the Autism Spectrum* for detailed practical examples and strategies (Williams and Wright 2004, 2007).

- *Picture Exchange Communication System (PECS®).* This is a system to help children's communication skills. The idea is to begin by helping the child to learn to exchange a card for a desired object. For example, the child might present the adult with a card with a picture of a cup of orange juice. The adult then quickly gives the drink in exchange. The child gradually learns to discriminate between different PECS pictures and eventually builds sentences with the cards. As the prompts are visual, language difficulties do not hamper its use. This system has however been found to improve language development. For more information, see www.pecs.org.uk

- *First/then (or now/next).* This is a simple strategy to encourage children to do certain activities, e.g. brush their teeth, or to help them to move on to a different activity. Usually it pairs activities together so that a liked activity comes after a less liked activity. For example, *first* brush teeth, *then* book. This works well with an A4 piece of card with a dividing line down the middle. On the left side at the top, the word First is written and on the right, the word Next at the top. Underneath you can attach the appropriate pictures or word cards with bluetac or Velcro. Pick something simple, quick and easily manageable the first few times you use this technique and when pointing to the card say, for example, '*First* teeth, *then* book.'

- Sometimes it is helpful to stay calm and watch and wait.

- Sometimes a change in time table will help.

- Understanding the needs of the child can often point towards different ideas for support.

Part 4

More Examples of
SOCIAL STORIES

WHY WE GO TO SCHOOL
A Story for Isabel Walker

One day at school, we visited the library. In the olden days, it was a school. Over the door of the library it says 'Learn or leave'.

This means that if the children didn't work hard and learn at school, they had to leave. Our school is a Primary School.

We are lucky. Teachers want us to learn, but they will not make us leave.

Children go to school for lots of reasons. Some of the reasons are:

- to play

- to be with friends and other adults

- to be independent from our parents.

The main reason we go to school is to learn. Learning is a good thing. There are lots of reasons why learning is good:

1. Learning makes us more interesting because we can talk about different things. I am good at listening carefully and remembering facts. My mum is amazed at some of the things I can remember. I know lots about King Henry, Queen Elizabeth and her cousin Mary.

2. Learning can help us find out what we enjoy and what we are good at. I enjoy stories and reading, like Belle and my sister, Lola.

3. Learning gives us useful skills that will help us look after ourselves when we grow up. There are lots of things we may learn to do on our own, like write shopping lists or letters, plan where to go on holiday or use computers.

4. Learning gives us useful skills to get a job we enjoy when we grow up. There are lots of great jobs, like being a teacher or a hairdresser or shop assistant.

The most important things we learn at school are reading, writing and numeracy. We learn these every day.

We still do lots of playing in class and at playtime. It is okay to play because we need a break from learning. Sometimes we learn when we are playing.

It helps to remember that if I learn lots at school I will be:

1. a more interesting person

2. able to do things I enjoy, like reading

3. able to look after myself when I grow up

4. able to get a job that I like when I grow up.

It is good to learn. I will try and learn as much as I can at school.

Why we like this Story: 'Why we go to school'

This Story and some of the following were written by Isabel's mum. They contain lots of positive information about Isabel's skills and she loves reading them. It has three parts and a title. The title describes the Story accurately and draws the child in. The introduction is really interesting, giving a local, historical perspective. The body of the Story shares accurate information about why we go to school. This is done with a very patient tone and uses only positive language. It answers the question implied in the title. It is tailored around Isabel's interests (history and reading), her age and ability level (aged 7) and applauds her skills: 'I am good at listening carefully and remembering facts'. This has the effect of helping her self-esteem and making it fun to read. It was presented originally with lots of photographs (17!) including pictures of her favourite historical figures, her favourite story characters, herself at school, her teachers and school. It is very much about the child, written largely in the first person (I) to reflect this.

The majority of the sentences, as in most Social Stories, are Descriptive Sentences, which give factual, objective information. There is a Descriptive Sentence, 'My mum is amazed at some of the things I can remember,' which gives her mum's viewpoint at the same time as boosting her self-esteem. Having provided information about why we go to school in the body of the Story, there is a short reminder about the four main points summarised in the conclusion. There is only one Coaching Sentence, which is the final sentence: 'I will try and learn as much as I can at school.' This works particularly well coming immediately after a Descriptive Sentence, which reinforces the message, 'It is good to learn.'

WORKING ON MY OWN
A Story for Isabel Walker

My name is Isabel. Miss Hughes is my teacher at school. Mrs Jones usually helps in class too. Sometimes I do 'school at home' with my mum.

Our teachers love to see our work and be impressed with what we have learnt. I have done lots of work that has impressed my teacher.

In class we play a lot and we learn in lots of fun ways together. Sometimes we are asked to sit down and work on our own.

I am good at sitting down to do my spelling or reading with my mum. I sit and listen well for carpet time. I wear my jacket and sit with Mrs Walsh.

I am brilliant at sitting down to play with my princesses or my doll's house.

Sometimes it's tricky for me to sit down, especially for numeracy and literacy. We do numeracy and literacy every day.

When teachers ask me to sit down and do some work, I will try to sit down and finish it.

Miss Hughes, Mrs Jones or someone else who is helping me will tell me what I have to do. It is important I know what to do. I can ask if I forget. If I am finding it tricky, I can ask for help. This is okay.

If I need a break, I can use a token on my wheel. I love this.

When it is finished I will be really pleased with myself.

If I stay in my seat and finish my work quickly, I can play or choose to do something else that is fun.

This means I can work on my own. It is called working independently. My teacher will be proud of me. She will tell my mum and Mum will be proud too.

Why we like this Story: 'Working on my own'

This Story was written for Isabel, who was finding it hard to make the transition from working with support to working on her own. She found it difficult to concentrate on numeracy and literacy in particular. Her mum wanted to keep the Story positive and so concentrated on Isabel's successes, which were related to examples where she could work successfully on her own. These are placed at the beginning of the Story to keep her interested and help her to feel good about herself: 'I am brilliant at sitting down to play with my princesses or my doll's house.'

Her mum uses some of her daughter's favourite words and phrases, which may not be relevant for other children with autism. For example, she liked the word 'tricky', meaning that this involved something that was difficult for her or a skill she was trying to acquire. She was keen to learn how to work on her own. The Coaching Sentence, 'When teachers ask me to sit down and do some work, I will try to sit down and finish it,' gives her a strategy to help her with this aim. There is also a Coaching Sentence for her teachers, 'Miss Hughes, Mrs Jones or someone else who is helping me will tell me what I have to do,' and two more which she developed herself: 'If I need a break, I can use a token on my wheel' (these were for short, favourite activities) and 'I can ask if I forget.' The Descriptive Sentence after this, 'This is okay', helps to reinforce the message. The conclusion to the Story reminds her that she has strategies to help her to achieve her aim of learning to work on her own. She is a child who responds really well to praise so the Descriptive Sentences, 'My teacher will be proud of me. She will tell my mum and Mum will be proud too,' are a great way to end the Story.

FOCUSING AND CONCENTRATING
A story for Isabel Walker

At school we have to do a lot of learning.

Some learning is fun.

Sometimes, we have to sit down and do some work. This means we have to focus and concentrate. Lots of children find this hard. And grown ups too!

Focusing means trying to do the things the teacher has asked us to do and trying not to be distracted.

Concentrating means thinking really hard so that we can understand what we are doing. Sometimes everything is easy and interesting and we don't even know we are concentrating. Sometimes our brains can feel muddled and tired when we are concentrating. This happens to everyone.

When our brains feel muddled and tired, the first thing to do is take a deep breath and try again. If this doesn't work, the best thing to do is ask the teacher for help. It is okay to ask teachers for help.

Teachers would like it if I could focus and concentrate for 5 minutes. This is just a short time. Then I can have a break and do another 5 minutes later.

If we spend more time focusing and concentrating, learning may get easier and we may be really proud of ourselves.

Why we like this Story: 'Focusing and concentrating'

This Story is an example of a Social Story which provides information about a life skill: 'focusing and concentrating'. It describes these skills as a function of the brain and the effects of how concentrating can make us feel muddled. It is written largely in the third person to make it clear that these are skills which apply to everyone. The sentences are mostly Descriptive, giving factual information. There are some simple Coaching Sentences, 'the first thing to do is take a deep breath and try again' and 'ask the teacher for help'. The Descriptive Sentence 'Teachers would like it if I could focus and concentrate for 5 minutes' is a reminder of the teacher's viewpoint. The concluding sentence is a summary of the focus of the topic and the positive outcome following the development of the skill.

TRYING HARD AT SWIMMING
A story for Isabel Walker

Swimming is lots of fun. My family enjoys going swimming together. We love Westport pool and going to Mary Jane's after for sausage, beans and toast and a chocolate milkshake – yum! I love this.

There are three reasons why swimming is great:

- It's fun.

- It helps to keep us fit and healthy.

- It helps to keeps us safe.

Most people find it difficult when they are first learning how to swim. There are lots of thing to do at the same time. They have to learn how to float, how to do different things with their arms and legs, how to breathe and to be brave and trust the teacher. I can do all these things.

I have swimming lessons on Friday at Thirsk. My teacher is Anna. She has two daughters. Once, when I swam really well, Anna gave me her old Mary Poppins doll – I love her.

I am good at swimming. I can swim 25 metres on my back in the big pool. I can swim front crawl in the big pool. I can swim underwater and collect things. I can jump in and touch the bottom in the deep end. At Westport, I can go down the big slide on my own and play in the waves without holding on. My mum and dad are so proud.

Even though I am good at swimming, it is important to keep improving. Then I can get even better and maybe be as good as Lola. To do that, I will do my best to *try hard*.

Trying hard means trying to keep going even when it feels difficult or it feels very tiring. This is okay. Sometimes children feel worried that they can't do something. Our teachers and parents only ask us to do difficult things when they know we can do it and we are safe. When Anna asks me to do something difficult, she is always there to make sure I am okay.

Trying hard means we get better at things and enjoy things more. *Trying hard* means that things get easier. *Trying hard* makes us feel proud of ourselves and what we can do. Anna and Mum are really pleased when I *try hard*, and impressed at what I can do. These are good feelings.

In my swimming lessons I swim six lengths in the big pool. I try to do the things Andrea asks me to do. Every week she will expect me to do a little bit more than I have done before. That way I will get better. This is called improving. If I try hard, I will improve a lot.

If Anna thinks I have tried hard, I can play in the little pool and I can have a treat from the vending machine. I like Magic Stars.

I will *try hard* at swimming. I will trust Anna because I know that she will look after me. Even when it is difficult, I will keep going. Then I will get even better at swimming and when I go on holiday to France, I will love all the swimming pools even more.

This is the swimming pool at the campsite we are going to in France:

Why we like this Story: 'Trying hard at swimming'

This Story has a clearly defined title. Isabel's parents wanted to encourage her to build on her success with swimming and wrote this Story to help her understand how to improve. The Story explains why trying hard helps with this. Most of the sentences are about Isabel's swimming achievements and her enjoyment of the activity. The photogaphs in it show examples of her skills and her happy face throughout. The Story helps her to recognise the benefits of trying hard. It uses a Descriptive Sentence, 'Sometimes children feel worried that they can't do something'. This sentence is written in the third person, which de-personalises it and normalises the emotion. It goes on to give reassurance: 'Our teachers and parents only ask us to do difficult things when they know we can do it and we are safe' and 'I will trust Anna because I know that she will look after me.'

Like most Stories, this one was edited several times. Isabel played a large part in the writing of her Stories, correcting them and also offering important additional information about her perspective, which was then included.

JOINING SCHOOL SWIMMING LESSONS
A story for Isabel Walker

This term I join school swimming lessons for 10 weeks. These are at Butterfield. All of the Year 4 children will go. Everybody will be at a different stage. Some will already be really good at swimming, and some won't have had lessons and will be learning in the little pool. I am good at swimming, but there will be better swimmers than me. This is okay, I can be proud of what I can do.

I can swim 25 metres in the big pool. I can swim different strokes, but backstroke is my favourite. I can swim underwater and collect things. I can jump in and touch the bottom in the deep end. In my swimming lessons I swim 10 or even 12 lengths in the big pool (I use a float for some of these). Mum, Dad and my teacher Anna are so proud.

Even though I am good at swimming, it is important to keep improving. Then I can get even better, safer and healthier and swimming will be easier. To do that, I will try to *stay confident* and *try hard*.

A few things will be different joining the school swimming lessons, especially staying focused in a group and going with lots of people. These are some things I will try to remember.

- Go to the toilet before we get on the coach to go to Thirsk.

- Be quick getting changed.

- Focus on my swimming.

- Listen carefully to the teacher and follow the instructions.

- Be confident so I can show everyone how good I am at swimming.

- Just a quick shower because there will lots of children needing a shower.

- Get dry and dressed as quickly as possible.

- No treat from the machine, but Mum will give me a good pack up.

Mrs Franklin will be there to help me, especially getting ready and dressed. Sarah and Emma will be my teachers. They will be making sure we are safe. This is okay.

It will be great fun to have swimming lessons with my friends from school. I am really looking forward to it.

Why we like this Story: 'Joining school swimming lessons'

This is a Story about preparing for a new experience. Although Isabel was a good swimmer, she had not been to swimming lessons with school before. Her mum spoke to the teachers to find out what might be different for Isabel in order to help her to prepare for this as knowing about new situations in advance was really helpful to her. As Isabel grew accustomed to Social Stories she found lists like those in this Story very useful.

HAPPY PLAYTIMES
A story for Isabel Walker

Playtime is one of my favourite things at school. I like playing with my friends. I like playing on the equipment, especially the new equipment.

It is great to run around and use some of my energy. This helps me focus and feel calm. When I am happy at playtime it makes me feel really good.

Sometimes children find playtimes difficult. It can be hard to find someone to play with and they feel a bit lonely.

If this happens, the best thing to do is to find a teacher or a dinner lady and ask them for help. They can help us to feel braver.

There are some other things that it is helpful to remember to have a happy playtime. At playtime, everyone goes out to play at the same time. Children start playing together quickly.

Sometimes some children get distracted or are a bit slower than the others and they get left behind.

This means the others have already started their games and it can be hard to join in. It is better to go out quickly, with everyone else. Then it will be easier to find friends to play with and have a happy playtime.

This is me playing with my friends at lunchtime.

I am allowed to take my princesses out at playtime. Some other children like to join in. I love it when they do this. I will try to only take them out occasionally or people will get bored with them. It is good when the princesses are a treat.

My sister is in the Junior playground. She is friendly and keeps an eye on me, but she likes to play with her own friends. They are older and play different games to me and talk about different things. This is okay and I will try to respect that. I can play and chat with her at home.

My friend Jack and I play great games together. But Jack sometimes wants to play with other children. This is okay and I will try to respect that. It's good to know the things I can try to do to have a happy playtime and that people are ready to help me if I need it.

Why we like this Story: 'Happy playtimes'

Playtimes can be problematic at times for most children. It is often difficult to understand the complex unwritten social rules, and particularly so for children with autism. This Story aims to identify some of the 'rules' that were most pertinent to Isabel at the time. It also gives her some information about why other people behave in certain ways using Descriptive Sentences: 'My sister…likes to play with her own friends. They are older and play different games to me and talk about different things.' It also gives her some ideas about what she can try to do to help using Coaching Sentences: 'This is okay and I will try to respect that. I can play and chat with her at home.' And when talking about her princess dolls, the Coaching Sentence 'I will try to only take them out occasionally or people will get bored with them' also adds a perspective phrase at the end.

Also this Story tries not to concentrate on Isabel's more difficult experiences at a personal level. Instead of focusing on her in the first person, it refers to 'children' more generally, for example 'Sometimes children find playtimes difficult. It can be hard to find someone to play with and they feel a bit lonely.' This then becomes a shared experience and helps her recognise that other children feel like this too.

The original Story had many photographs of her in the playground having a great time, including sitting chatting to others with princess dolls and skipping happily on her own. This helps to keep the Story positive and adds to her enjoyment of the Story.

TAKING NEW MEDICINE
A story for Isabel Walker

I have epilepsy. Epilepsy is to do with your brain.

Different bits of your brain work different bits of your body. Your brain sends lots of messages to different parts of your body to tell it what to do. If you have epilepsy, these messages get a bit mixed up and then you have seizures.

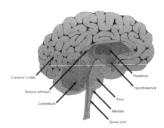

I have seizures. It means that my brain just stops for a few seconds. I go quiet and still and my eyes look a bit funny. These are called absence seizures. Then I just carry on what I was doing. Most of the time I don't even notice I am having a seizure.

My mum and dad are in charge of giving me my medicine. I have it twice a day. This stops me having nearly all my seizures. If I didn't take medicine, I would have LOADS of seizures. This would stop me doing all sorts of things, like playing, eating, running, learning, listening to stories… It wouldn't be much fun and life would be hard. It is good that my medicine makes things better.

I am good at taking my medicine. I have pink medicine in the morning and at bedtime, in a little cup. It tastes okay. At bedtime I have another medicine that doesn't taste so nice, but I am brave and swallow it quickly.

I need to take a new medicine. It's purple. I need to take it twice a day, at the same time as the pink medicine. I will have this from a spoon to start with. Each week I will have more. In the end, I will drink it from a cup too.

It is important to take the new medicine, as this makes my seizures go away. I will be good at taking it and will get used to it very quickly.

Why we like this Story: 'Taking new medicine'

This Story was written to give accurate, reassuring information about Isabel's epilepsy and the reasons for a change in medication. It gives simple, clear, factual information about her seizures and is written at the appropriate level for her. It is written very positively and reminds her of all of the fun things her medication allows her do. Importantly, it is also very honest and recognises that one of her medicines 'doesn't taste so nice', however it quickly praises her, adding, 'but I am brave and swallow it quickly'.

Acknowledgements

We would like to thank Isabel for sharing her wonderful Stories to be included in this guide. They are all great examples of Social Stories. Her mum, Elaine, wrote most of these Social Stories with her.

FINDING OUT ABOUT ARCHBISHOP HOLGATE SIXTH FORM

When students in Year 11 leave school they sometimes go to college or Sixth Form.

When I leave school I may choose to go to college or Sixth Form.

On the 21 November, at 7 o'clock there is an open evening at Archbishop Holgate Sixth Form.

At the open evening I may meet tutors, I may meet other Year 11 students and I may find out about different courses I could study.

I enjoy history, media and science – especially astronomy.

It is good to learn about things that I'm interested in.

Mum and the tutors could help me to choose a course that I may enjoy.

There is a café area at Archbishop Holgate Sixth Form, where students can buy drinks and snacks. It may be a good place to meet other students.

There are private study areas at Archbishop Holgate Sixth Form where students go to work quietly. It is good to find a quiet place to think and study.

I will find out more information when I go to visit Archbishop Holgate Sixth Form's open evening. My mum and Mrs Bee will come with me. They think it will be good to have a look around and learn more about the Sixth Form. It may help me to decide if I would like to go to study there in September and which course I may enjoy.

It is a good idea to go to the open evening.

Why we like this Story: 'Finding out about Archbishop Holgate Sixth Form'

This is a good example of a Social Story that gives information in advance about going somewhere different. Simon was finishing at his school in July and deciding about the options available to him at Sixth Form. He was extremely anxious about this. His mum and his teachers wrote this Story and added pictures of the Sixth Form to offer him some information and reassurance prior to his open evening visit. Young people with autism frequently find it hard to imagine new situations so a Story with photographs like this one often helps to reduce their anxiety.

Other similar Stories were written by the local specialist ASD teachers about other college open evenings.

VISITING THE DENTIST

Dentists look after children's teeth. Dentists help keep teeth clean and healthy.

Here are some dentists.

Dentists work in a building called a surgery.

Sometimes there are toys for children to play with.

The dentist has special equipment to help look at children's teeth.

The chair can move up and down, to help the dentist see the teeth.

This is a mirror to help the dentist count teeth.

Children try to keep their mouths open so the dentist can look at their teeth.

There may be a bright light to help the dentist see the teeth.

That's okay, if it's too bright children can wear dark glasses.

Some dentists wear plastic gloves and masks. It helps protect children from germs.

Sometimes children wear a bib.

The dentist likes to look at teeth and help children to look after them.

Children can ask the dentist questions about things they see and hear if they are not sure what they are.

The dentist will be very happy when children try to keep their teeth clean and healthy.

It is good to visit the dentist.

Why we like this Story: 'Visiting the dentist'

This is another Social Story giving reassuring information concerning a new situation that may cause anxiety. It provides some factual information about visiting the dentist. It is a Story that could easily be changed to include more personal information if required.

WHY WE DO HOMEWORK

During the week I usually go to my school.

At school my teacher sometimes gives me work or some reading to do at home.

When I do my homework, I might learn new things. I like learning about the Egyptians and about Japan.

Doing homework helps me to practise what I have been learning at school. Then I can show my teacher that I understand what we are working on.

Homework also helps me to remember some of the new things I have learned at school.

Homework is a good way of showing how well I am doing in my lessons to Mum and Dad.

When I am given homework, I will try to do it on time and do the best that I can.

When I finish my homework then I get to decorate my homework folder with an extra sticker.

Doing homework is a good idea and will make people at home and school proud of me.

Why we like this Story: 'Why we do homework'

This Story provides information about homework. It answers the question in the title about 'Why do we do homework', in a very clear, friendly non-judgemental way. It is very positive and is personalised towards the young person, encouraging him by referring to his favourite topics, Egyptians and Japan. Most of the sentences are Descriptive Sentences. There is one Coaching Sentence, 'When I am given homework, I will try to do it on time and do the best that I can.' The Descriptive Sentence at the end also provides a very positive ending.

HOW TO TAKE TESTS

Sometimes we have tests at school so that our teachers can find out what we have learnt.

Usually we do tests in answer booklets.

When taking a test it is a good idea to read the questions carefully and think about the answer before writing.

Some questions are easy and some may be harder.

I will try and answer all the easy questions first and then try the hard questions.

Some children have extra time to take tests, this is a good idea. I can have extra time too.

If I have time at the end of the test I can check my answers.

In maths tests I can get extra marks if I show my workings out.

This helps my teachers to understand how I have worked out my answer.

Taking tests can be okay. They are just one way of showing what I know.

Why we like this Story: 'How to take tests'

This Story is an example of using a Social Story to prepare for a new experience. It provides some information about why we take tests. It answers the 'wh' questions of which questions to answer first, what to do and why we take tests. It offers reassuring information: 'Taking tests can be okay. They are just one way of showing what I know.'

WAITING TO ASK THE TEACHER A QUESTION

I like to going to school and learning about different things like astronomy and mythical creatures and Greek heroes. *(Descriptive)*

I have lots of questions to ask. *(Descriptive)*

When I have a question for the teacher, I may put up my hand. *(Descriptive)*

When the teacher is helping someone else, I will try to wait patiently and quietly. *(Coaching)*

When it is my turn, he will ask me about my question. *(Descriptive)*

I will try to do good waiting. *(Coaching)*

Waiting quietly shows that we respect and care about the people around us. *(Descriptive)*

If I do good waiting the teacher will try to answer my question. *(Descriptive)*

He will be pleased that I tried to wait quietly. *(Descriptive)*

Why we like this Story: 'Waiting to ask the teacher a question'

This is a straightforward Story that opens with positive things that the child likes to do in school. It explains in simple ways how to ask questions in class and about 'good waiting'. It does all this very positively and without criticism. It makes good use of the word 'try', because sometimes 'good waiting' is difficult. Also sometimes the teacher may not be able to answer the question, so the teacher will 'try to answer my question'. This is accurate and allows for the fact the teacher may not immediately know the answer.

GOING TO FLAMINGO LAND

On Friday 11 July I'm going on the school visit to Flamingo Land.

I don't need to wear a school uniform, it's okay to wear casual clothes. Everyone will try to take a packed lunch and a waterproof jacket, in case it rains.

After register, the teacher will tell everyone when it's time to get on the bus. The bus usually takes everyone to Flamingo Land.

At Flamingo Land there are lots of things to do. I may like to go on the rides, I may like to visit the animals, I may like to walk around and chat to people from my school.

When people go on the rides, they usually line up. They get on the ride when it's their turn. If I choose to go on a ride, I will try to line up. It's good to take turns.

There will usually be an adult nearby. If I need help, it's okay to ask an adult from my school.

At lunchtime it's okay to eat my packed lunch. It would be good to eat my lunch with a friend.

If I choose to visit the animals I may learn lots of unusual things about them.

Flamingo Land has signposts to help people find all the interesting things they may like to look at.

When the visit is finished the teachers will ask everyone to get back on the bus. The bus usually takes us back to school.

When I arrive home, I may be able to tell my family about the things I saw and what I liked best at Flamingo Land.

It's good to visit places with my friends from York High School.

Why we like this Story: 'Going to Flamingo Land'

It is a good example of a Story used to prepare a young person for a new experience. It answers numerous questions about what is likely to happen on the visit and should reduce some of his anxiety.

I AM A KIND, INTELLIGENT PERSON

My name is Jim and I love to play with Lego blocks. *(Descriptive)* They are my favourite thing to play with at break time and I usually build some very interesting things. *(Descriptive)* One time I built an aeroplane with four wings and a pilot. It was really good! *(Descriptive)* Another time I built a tower that was almost as tall as I am. *(Descriptive)* Another time I built a robot and that was my favourite thing that I have built so far. *(Descriptive)* My dad says that I am really intelligent.

Sometimes, Tom and Jen come to play with the Lego too. They love playing with Lego. *(Descriptive)* Mrs White said that it is very kind of me to let them play with the Lego. *(Descriptive)*

This was a kind thing to do. *(Descriptive)*

I am a kind, intelligent person. *(Descriptive)*

Why we like this Story: 'I am a kind, intelligent person'

Jim is a boy with Asperger syndrome who attends a mainstream primary school. He is very intelligent but has had a number of issues with interacting with his classmates in the past. These all seem to stem from his need to follow set routines. His teachers have noted that Jim has made a big effort to be more flexible lately and his teacher wanted to write a Social Story praising this. Writing Stories to praise a new skill or achievement is really helpful for encouraging children and developing their self-esteem. It is a Story which describes his favourite activities and achievements. There is no need for Coaching Sentences in this Story. This is an example of writing a Social Story to applaud a child's achievement.

SPIDERMAN IS A FILM CHARACTER

I am good at telling people facts about superheroes.

Spiderman is my favourite superhero. I like him because he is brave and strong and he can shoot webs from his wrists.

Spiderman is a character who was made up for a comic by a man called Stan Lee. I will try to remember that Spiderman isn't a real person. He is an actor in a costume who pretends to be the film character.

The person who dresses up as Spiderman in the films is called Tobey Maguire. He is an actor from America. The film makers have special effects to make it look like he can shoot webs and climb buildings. He can't really do these things. It is just pretend. It would be very dangerous if he tried to climb buildings in real life. Everyone wants to keep him safe.

Sometimes I wear a Spiderman costume so I can pretend to be Spiderman some of the time. I can pretend to fire webs. It is fun.

When I want to climb, I will try to climb in safe places.

I may go to the climbing wall at the Sports Centre with my dad or on the climbing frame at the park with my big brother. Then I can stay safe like Tobey Maguire who plays Spiderman.

Spiderman is a great film character!

Why we like this Story: 'Spiderman is a film character'

This was written for a boy who loved Spiderman. When he was dressed in his Spiderman costume his parents worried that he thought he was Spiderman and could take on super powers. He has Asperger syndrome. He found it hard sometimes to differentiate between real and pretend. This Story focuses really well on his interest in Spiderman but gives very clear information that he isn't real and that the film makers use special effects to give the appearance he has special powers. It also gives safe alternatives such as where he can go to climb safely.

USING WORDS THAT PEOPLE LIKE

When children are together at break times and lunchtimes, they usually chat and talk. Children talk about their interests such as cars and games. This is fun.

Sometimes children are excited and use lots of words to make them sound clever and funny. Sometimes children use rude swear words to sound clever and funny. Words can be funny and clever without being rude. In conversations, some children are offended when they hear rude words. They may be embarrassed or upset. Some children do not like to join in conversations when others are using rude words.

If children are happy, they are more likely to join the conversation. Teachers like it when children chat happily. This is great and everyone is happy.

At break times and lunchtimes, I will try to use words that are clever and funny and avoid rude swear words.

Why we like this Story: 'Using words that people like'

This was written for a boy who was using swear words when he was with his peers. His teachers believed that he thought that he was being funny when he did this because his peers often laughed. They used this Story to try to help him to understand that some people find swear words upsetting and that he could still be funny by using different words. The Story stays positive whilst providing him with clear factual social information.

Part 5

Appendices

These template are available to download from
www.jkp.com/catalogue/book/9781785921216

A TEMPLATE FOR MAKING SENSE OF A CHILD'S BEHAVIOUR AND PLANNING WAYS TO HELP

1. What is the problem?

_____

What does the child do (or not do) that you would like to be different? Be specific and not general (e.g. refuses to put shoes on rather than problems getting dressed).

2. Why does the child behave in this way at present?

_____

The shaded sections are to do with ASD.

Mindblindness Can they see others' points of view or understand feelings and needs of others in this situation? Do they realise they need to communicate their needs to someone?	
Getting the gist Does the child understand the social meaning of the situation? Do they know what to expect and how to respond to this social situation? Do they need help with this?	

Communication Do they understand the need to communicate, what to say and why? Do they need help to explain their actions, which may be very plausible to themselves?	
Imagination Does the child think imaginatively? Does this affect their ability to play? Have they interpreted something literally? Is the problem to do with lack of ability to plan?	
Sensory experiences Is the problem associated with sensory experiences (the smell, sound, feel, taste, colour or look of something)? Are they frightened or in pain? Are their preoccupations interfering with learning?	
Preoccupations and routine Is it to do with a need for routine or habits? Is there a need to be in control? Has there been a change of routine at home or at school?	
Situations and settings Where does it happen? Where does it not happen? Who is around when it happens?	
Triggers and timings When does it happen? What are the timings in relation to other things? When does it not happen? What is the trigger? Is it related to anxiety or the child's temperament? Is there anything that might be upsetting the child (e.g. memories, illness, tiredness, boredom)?	
Responses and reinforcers How have others responded? Does something happen after the behaviour that is important? How does it affect the behaviour in the future? What are the benefits of this behaviour? For you? For the child? (Rack your brains, there usually are some.)	

3. What does the child or young person need help with?

_____

Now that you have a better understanding of why the child might be behaving in this way you can decide what he or she needs help with. For example, refusing to put shoes on might be because the shoes are the wrong colour, have buttons on, etc., or because they prefer the routine of getting dressed first or having a specific person to help them with their shoes, or the shoes hurt, or they don't see the point of wearing shoes, etc. The list is endless! Having discovered the reasons why the behaviour occurs will helps you to be clear about your aim.

4. *What* specifically do you hope will change?

_____

Will the child benefit, or you, or both? You are preparing the child for the future as well as dealing with the present. Does it meet the SMART criteria (Specific, Measurable, Achievable, Realistic, Time limited)?

STEP-BY-STEP FLOWCHART

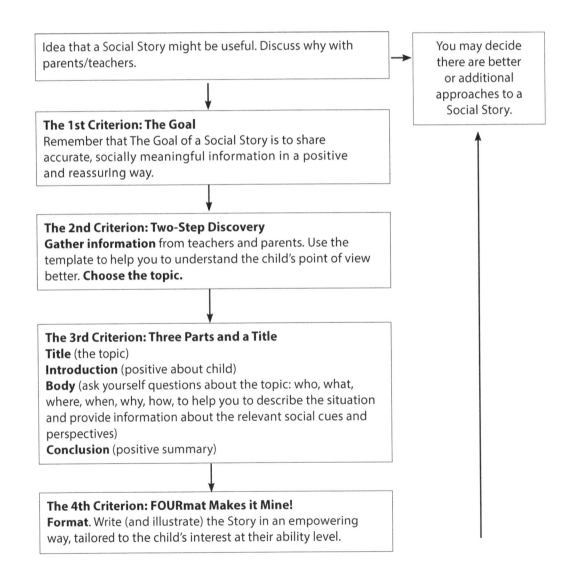

Idea that a Social Story might be useful. Discuss why with parents/teachers.

You may decide there are better or additional approaches to a Social Story.

The 1st Criterion: The Goal
Remember that The Goal of a Social Story is to share accurate, socially meaningful information in a positive and reassuring way.

The 2nd Criterion: Two-Step Discovery
Gather information from teachers and parents. Use the template to help you to understand the child's point of view better. **Choose the topic.**

The 3rd Criterion: Three Parts and a Title
Title (the topic)
Introduction (positive about child)
Body (ask yourself questions about the topic: who, what, where, when, why, how, to help you to describe the situation and provide information about the relevant social cues and perspectives)
Conclusion (positive summary)

The 4th Criterion: FOURmat Makes it Mine!
Format. Write (and illustrate) the Story in an empowering way, tailored to the child's interest at their ability level.

The 5th Criterion: Five Factors Define Voice and Vocabulary
Factors to keep the Story positive and accurate:
> pronouns: are all sentences written in the first and/or third person?
> ensure it has a positive and patient tone (no negatives)
> use relevant information from the person's past, present or future
> is every sentence and word literally accurate?
> is every verb selected to be closest to its intended meaning?

The 6th Criterion: Six Questions Guide Story Development
Answer questions relevant to the topic. Who, what, where, when, why and how

The 7th Criterion: Seven is About Sentences
Sentence types in Social Stories:
Descriptive: describe information factually, objectively or that everybody knows and describe the thoughts, feelings or beliefs of people and reinforce points in the Story
Coaching: describe or suggest responses, e.g. 'I will try to eat quietly'

The 8th Criterion: A GR-EIGHT Formula!
To keep the balance of Sentences correct, add up all the Descriptive Sentences and divide that number by the number of Coaching Sentences. It can be called a Social Story if the answer is greater than or equal to 2.

The 9th Criterion: Nine to Refine
Refine. Use the checklist.

The 10th Criterion: Ten Guides to Implementation
Implement. Edit, prepare and read the Story. Then review it.

CHECKLIST

A Social Story follows certain 'rules'. Many people think these are complicated. They are not. They are very simple and designed to make sure that the Social Story is a positive experience for the child or young person. Another way of looking at this is that they are a checklist for making sure that your Social Story has a good chance of being helpful and nurturing to the young person. There are two versions; the first five-page version offers more detail.

1. The Goal

✓ Does your Social Story share accurate social information?

✓ Does the Story have an overall patient and reassuring quality?

2. Two-Step Discovery

✓ Have you discussed this with a parent/carer?

✓ Have you discussed this with another person who knows the child well?

✓ Have you made at least two observations of the child in the relevant setting (as objective onlooker and from the perspective of the child)?

✓ Is there one clear focus or topic?

✓ Is this for the child's benefit?

3. Three Parts and a Title

Does the Story have the following?

✓ **title**

✓ **introduction**

✓ **body**

✓ **conclusion**

4. FOURmat Makes it Mine!

Are the text and illustrations written and presented in a way consistent with the child's ability, talents and interests so that will enhance its meaning and engage the child?

✓ **learning style**

✓ **attention span**

✓ **level of understanding**

✓ **language**

✓ **interests**

5. Five Factors Define Voice and Vocabulary

✓ **Are *all* sentences written in the first (I) and/or third person (she, it, they)?**

'You…' (second person) statements can make the Story too directive, so are not used.

Where it is necessary to explain negative behaviours always refer to the third person (not to the child). Use a 'learning vantage point' such as 'Sometimes children may speak whilst someone else is still talking. This is called interrupting. With practice children learn when to talk and when to listen.'

The first person is never used in reference to a negative, ineffective or undesirable behaviour. For example, rather than using 'I should not interrupt the head teacher when she is speaking in assembly', instead use 'Children try to listen when the head teacher is talking to the group in assembly.'

✓ **Does the Story have a positive and patient tone?**

Avoid negative phrasing and negative verbs, for example:

- should/shouldn't
- supposed to/mustn't
- ought/ought to know better
- bad/naughty
- never/always
- can't/don't.

✓ **Have you used relevant information from the child's past, present or future?**

✓ **Is the Social Story literally accurate (every word, phrase or sentence can be interpreted literally without changing the intended meaning)?**

✓ **Are verbs carefully selected to be closest to the intended meaning?**

Try to be accurate in meaning, especially when using verbs. For example, 'Jane will get the food from the supermarket' – a better sentence would be 'Jane will buy the food from the supermarket.' N.B. Analogies and/or metaphors or idioms may be used if they are known to be understood by the child.

6. Six Questions Guide Story Development

✓ **Does the Story answer questions relevant to the specific topic?**

7. Seven is About Sentences

✓ **Does your Social Story have at least one Descriptive Sentence?**

Ensure that the balance of Sentences is correct. Add the number of Descriptive Sentences and divide that by the number of Coaching Sentences. The answer should be greater than or equal to 2.

8. A GR-EIGHT Formula!

✓ **Does your Social Story have very few Coaching Sentences (less than a third of the total number of sentences)?**

The reason for this is to 'describe' the social situation rather than telling the child what to do. Social Stories have a reassuring tone.

9. Nine to Refine

✓ **Has there been more than one draft of your Story (to show you are editing and revising)?**

10. Ten Guides to Implementation

Preparing to present the Story

✓ **Does the child understand the Story?**

✓ **Have you prepared carefully the way in which the Story was to be presented?**

Discuss the practicalities of presentation, including:

- Who will introduce it to the child?

- Who reads it with the child?

- Where (include any changes or adaptations in the environment)?

- When?

- How?

- How often?
- Confidentiality.

Reading the Story

✓ **Was the Story consistently presented in a confidential, comfortable setting with a positive tone?**

When you deliver it ensure you have:

- prepared the child for the Social Story (before it is used)
- made sure that the child is ready and receptive (e.g. in a good mental and physical space) so they will enjoy the Social Story or get something positive from it
- used checklist item 10 regularly, checking and reviewing with colleagues that the Story is helping and adapting as necessary.

CHECKLIST (SHORT VERSION)

1. The Goal

✓ Does your Social Story share accurate social information?

✓ Does the Story have an overall patient and reassuring quality?

2. Two-Step Discovery

✓ Have you discussed this with a parent/carer?

✓ Have you discussed this with another person who knows the child well?

✓ Have you made at least two observations of the child in the relevant setting (as objective onlooker and from the perspective of the child)?

✓ Is there one clear focus or topic?

✓ Is this for the child's benefit?

3. Three Parts and a Title

Does the Story have the following?

✓ title

✓ introduction

✓ body

✓ conclusion

4. FOURmat Makes it Mine!

Are the text and illustrations written and presented in a way consistent with the child's ability that will enhance its meaning or engage the child?

✓ learning style

✓ attention span

✓ level of understanding

✓ language

✓ interests

5. Five Factors Define Voice and Vocabulary

✓ Are all sentences written in the first (I) and/or third person (she, it, they)?

✓ Does the Story have a positive and patient tone?

✓ Have you used relevant information from the child's past, present or future?

✓ Is the Social Story literally accurate (every word, phrase or sentence can be interpreted literally without changing the intended meaning)?

✓ Are verbs carefully selected to be closest to the intended meaning?

6. Six Questions Guide Story Development

✓ Does the Story answer questions relevant to the specific topic?

7. Seven is About Sentences

✓ **Does your Social Story have at least one Descriptive Sentence?**

Ensure that the balance of Sentences is correct. Add the number of Descriptive Sentences and divide that by the number of Coaching Sentences. The answer should be greater than or equal to 2.

8. A GR-EIGHT Formula!

✓ **Does your Social Story have few Coaching Sentences (less than a third of the total number of sentences)?**

9. Nine to Refine

✓ **Has there been more than one draft of your Story (to show you are editing and revising)?**

10. Ten Guides to Implementation

Preparing to present the Story

✓ **Does the child understand the Story?**

✓ **Did you prepare carefully the way in which the Story was to be presented?**

Reading the Story

✓ **Was the Story consistently presented in a confidential, comfortable setting with a positive tone?**

DEFINITIONS OF TERMS

ASD Autism spectrum disorders, which include autism, Asperger syndrome and atypical autism.

Audience This is the person for whom the Story is written (Audience is always capitalised when referring to a Social Story.)

Author This is the person or people who write the Story. (Author is always capitalised when referring to a Social Story.)

Mindblindness describes being blind to the mind of others or struggling to make accurate guesses about how someone else thinks or feels (see TOM).

Picture Exchange Communication System (PECS˙) A system that helps a child learn to initiate communication or make requests initially and builds this gradually over time into sentences. For more information, see www.pecs.org.uk

Social Story™ TM stands for Trade Mark. Social Stories refers to Social Stories as defined by Carol Gray.

Team This is all of those people working together on behalf of the Audience. (Team is always capitalised when referring to a Social Story.)

TOM 'Theory of Mind' is a term that some professionals use to describe how one person can have a guess or a theory about what is in the mind of another person. They can guess about someone else's thoughts or attitudes or experiences.

Visual time tables Pictures that describe the sequence of activities the child may do in a day or part of a routine. They might be on a laminated strip with Velcro so that items can be 'posted' in a box when completed.

REFERENCES

Gray, C. (2010) *The New Social Stories Book*. Arlington, TX: Future Horizons Incorporated.

Gray, C. (2015) *The New Social Story Book, Revised and Expanded 15th Anniversary Edition*. Arlington, TX: Future Horizons Incorporated.

Gray, C. and Leigh White, A. (2001) *My Social Stories Book*. London: Jessica Kingsley Publishers.

Marshall, D., Wright, B., Allgar, V., Adamson, J., *et al.* (2016) 'Social Stories in mainstream schools for children with autism spectrum disorder: a feasibility randomised controlled trial.' *BMJ Open* 6(8): e011748.

Vermeulen, P. (2012) *Autism as Context Blindness*. Lenexa, KS: AAPC Publishing.

Williams, C. and Wright, B. (2004) *How to Live with Autism and Asperger Syndrome: Practical Strategies for Parents and Teachers*. London: Jessica Kingsley Publishers.

Wright, B., Marshall, D., Collingridge Moore, D., Ainsworth, H., Hackney, L., Adamson, J. *et al.* (2014) 'Autism Spectrum Social Stories in Schools Trial (ASSSIST): study protocol for a feasibility randomised controlled trial analysing clinical and cost-effectiveness of Social Stories in mainstream schools.' *BMJ Open* 4(7), e005952.

Wright, B., Marshall, D., Adamson, J., Ainsworth, H., *et al.* (2016) 'Social Stories to alleviate challenging behaviour and social difficulties exhibited by children with autism spectrum disorder in mainstream schools: design of a manualised training toolkit and feasibility study for a cluster randomised controlled trial with nested qualitative and cost-effectiveness components.' *Health Technol Assess* 20(6).

Wright, B. and Williams, C. (2007) *Intervention and Support for Parents and Carers of Children and Young People on the Autism Spectrum: A Resource for Trainers*. London: Jessica Kingsley Publishers.

INDEX

Chris Williams is a Clinical Psychologist and **Barry Wright** is a Consultant Child and Adolescent Psychiatrist. They have both worked for the NHS with children with ASDs and their families for over 20 years. They are the authors of *How to Live with Autism and Asperger Syndrome: Practical Strategies for Parents and Professionals* and *Intervention and Support for Parents and Carers of Children and Young People on the Autism Spectrum: A Resource for Trainers*, both published by JKP. They both live in North Yorkshire, UK.

CPI Antony Rowe
Eastbourne, UK
December 20, 2024